PRESERVING WEALTH

THE NEXT GENERATION

THE DEFINITIVE GUIDE TO PROTECTING, INVESTING, AND TRANSFERRING WEALTH.

JACK LUMSDEN, MBA, CFP®

Tellwell Talent
www.tellwell.ca

ISBN
978-0-2288-1094-0 (Paperback)
978-0-2288-1095-7 (eBook)

In memory of
William Lumsden
Sybil Lumsden (nee Aiken)
Rick Dowling
Mike Farrauto
Frank Peruzzi

DISCLOSURES

Jack Lumsden is a Senior Wealth Advisor with Assante Financial Management Ltd. ("AFM").

The material provided in this book is for general information and is subject to change without notice. The views and opinions expressed in this book are those of the author only and do not necessarily reflect the opinions of AFM. Furthermore, they should not be considered as product endorsement or for promotional purposes by AFM. Every effort has been made to compile this material from reliable sources however no warranty can be made as to its accuracy or completeness. Insurance products and services are provided through Assante Estate and Insurance Services Inc.

AFM is a member of the Mutual Fund Dealers Association of Canada ("MFDA") and MFDA Investor Protection Corporation. Mutual funds are provided through AFM and only those services offered through AFM are covered by the MFDA Investor Protection Corporation.

Please contact Jack at 905-332-5503 or visit www.jacklumsden.com to discuss your particular circumstances.

Table of Contents

About the Author

Jack Lumsden, MBA, CFP®, is a financial advisor with over twenty years of experience. He has enjoyed building a strong career and loyal client base. In addition to helping clients preserve and transfer their wealth, he focuses on those who are or will be making the transition from their working years to retirement with the need to develop a lifelong income and cash-flow strategy from the financial assets they have accumulated.

A lifelong resident of Burlington, Jack dedicates much of his spare time to staying active and coaching high school football. Spending time with family is another of his core values. He enjoys attending sports events with his son, Connor, and country music concerts with daughter, Paige, while he and his wife, Sandi, like to travel with friends and explore new destinations.

Jack's education includes a BBA from Wilfrid Laurier University (where he met Sandi) and an MBA from McMaster University. He is also a CERTIFIED FINANCIAL PLANNER® or CFP® professional.

How to Contact Jack Lumsden, MBA, CFP®

Jack Lumsden, MBA, CFP®
Senior Wealth Advisor
Assante Financial Management Ltd,

Phone:	905.332.5503
Email:	jlumsden@assante.com
Web Site:	www.jacklumsden.com

If, after reading this book, you have any questions or would like to arrange an appointment to review your current financial situation, please call or email us.

Chapter 1

INTRODUCTION—MEET THE CAST

It was the usual opening day for our father's summer cottage, the May 24 weekend. As I sat on the deck that overlooked the bay, I thought back over the history of our cottage and our family in Honey Harbour.

Dad's parents built their cottage in 1922. In those days, it took thirteen bumpy hours by car to get there from the city. It was worth it, they say, even with five noisy boys roughhousing most of the way. Today that same ride takes just an hour and a half from Toronto, most of the time, although the last ten minutes are still bumpy.

My parents were in their late thirties before they could afford their own land in Honey Harbour. They found a beautiful spot about a mile north of the Musquois River, and they used to spend an hour getting there from the marina by boat. There's still no road access to the cottage, but with today's faster boats, we can make the same trip in under twenty minutes.

Some relatives and family friends had also bought land nearby and built their own cottages, so over the years, my brother, sister, and I had plenty of friends with whom to pass the time swimming, water-skiing, boating, and windsurfing—all the experiences that made life on the bay so enjoyable.

As adults, we've all brought our spouses and children to our cottages as well, and they too have fallen in love with Honey Harbour.

On opening weekend, we usually celebrate the arrival of another great season, but this time there was a lot of sadness in the air. Our father had died over the winter. He'd been very sick, but still it was hard to accept that he was gone. And here we were at the cottage he'd built and had now left to us kids.

Of course, we weren't kids any more. I'm forty, and I've been married to Sandra for ten years. We have a three-year-old son named Connor, and a baby girl named Paige. My older brother, David, is fifty and married to a very patient woman named Alice. They have two kids of their own, a couple of wild teenagers named Scott and Jan. My sister, Sally, was the baby of the family, but even she's thirty-five now and still single. I like to tease her about both.

We all used to get together with my cousin's family every Saturday morning at alternating cottages for a big breakfast, and we decided to keep up the tradition started by our parents.

The first Saturday breakfast was at our cottage, with David and me on cooking detail. Aunt Lorraine came over with my cousin Mark, who's about sixty-three. Uncle Jim had passed away seven years earlier.

We had our normal discussions regarding what had happened to the cottages over the winter, what work we needed to do, and how it would fit into everyone's vacation plans for the summer. Aunt Lorraine was the one who first brought up the subject of Dad's will. He had left everything equally to we three kids, and it was an inheritance that included mutual funds, an annuity, limited partnerships, a house, and, of course, this cottage.

Aunt Lorraine wondered what we planned to do with our "sudden wealth," and when no one had any specific plans, she suggested that we talk to our old family friend across the bay. We kids had all called him "Uncle Wayne" for as long as I could remember, even though we weren't related. He and his wife lived in Honey Harbour all summer and travelled to Florida and Europe for part of the winter each year.

According to Aunt Lorraine, he had helped her sort out her financial affairs when she was widowed and had continued to give her good financial advice.

Sally wasn't sure she wanted to talk about finances at all. "I feel guilty about the money I've received so far, and even about being here at the cottage," she said. "It just doesn't feel right to have Dad's money and the things he worked so hard to get."

David nodded, and I understood what she meant too. However, Aunt Lorraine said she'd spoken with Dad many times about his estate. Sure, he'd done a lot of careful financial planning, but he also had lived a good lifestyle and had no regrets. He would want us to enjoy the money, she said, and to use it wisely.

That won Sally over. "I guess we should do some planning. Let's talk to Uncle Wayne."

I had to borrow some tools from Uncle Wayne in order to put our floating dock in the water, so I told the others I would ask his advice when I saw him later that day.

Aunt Lorraine turned to Mark and said, "You should listen in on any advice he gives."

Mark looked a little shocked. "What are you talking about? You're not sick, are you?"

"No, I'm fine," she said. "Don't worry. It's just that I was golfing with Uncle Wayne last week, and we started talking about how hefty estate taxes are. He mentioned that when someone receives an inheritance, they don't pay tax on the proceeds; however, any tax owing does need to be paid by the estate of the person who passed away. He said that one way to pay as little estate tax as possible is to give some of my money away before I die. I figure I have a few extra dollars that I don't need, so I want to give you some of your inheritance now, but I don't want you to blow it."

"Gee, Mom, are you sure you can afford it?"

She smiled and answered that she could and would still be able to live very well for the next twenty years, and maybe even longer.

I said I would call Mark after my visit with Uncle Wayne.

WHAT TO DO FIRST?

I went across the bay in our tin boat to borrow the tools from our parents' good friend, Uncle Wayne.

Uncle Wayne met me at the dock and helped tie the boat so we could go up to his cottage for our customary beer. We talked about my father for a while, and how much we'd both miss him. Uncle Wayne laughed and said he'd especially miss golfing with Dad, since he was the only person he could beat every time at the Honey Harbour Golf & Country Club. I brought up our dilemma, that we all didn't know what to do with our new-found wealth.

Uncle Wayne said, "I thought you might ask me about this, and I've done some thinking about it. Do you three still plan to get together with Mark for breakfast every Saturday morning this summer?"

"How did you know Mark needs financial advice too?" I asked.

He mentioned his conversation with Aunt Lorraine and suggested that we use our Saturday morning breakfast ritual to discuss strategies for our inheritances. I felt that was a good idea, since weekends were designated as family time when everyone could use the cottage. We knew we eventually had to sell it in order to divide up its value for the estate, but in the meantime, we had agreed to share all the weekends and take individual weeks for our holidays during the summer.

Next, Uncle Wayne wanted to know what everyone had done with their inheritance so far. I answered that we'd each received some cash, and that mine was sitting in the bank. I didn't know about the others.

"I see I have my work cut out for me," said Uncle Wayne. "Okay, first make sure that none of you say a word to anyone about inheriting. People will come out of the woodwork with all sorts of business schemes, and they may possibly want to borrow money. In a worst-case scenario, you may become a target for criminals who think that you are better off than you really are. Today, modesty can be a virtue, and it's certainly the safest way to go.

"Next," he continued, "be sure to tell David, Sally, and Mark that for the short term, until we come up with individual long-term plans for each of you, they should be looking both at the safety of the money and at the interest rates they can earn.

"If you deposit the money at your bank or trust company in a savings or chequing account, it's guaranteed by the Canada Deposit Insurance Corporation (CDIC), but only to a limit of $100,000 per person per financial institution (bank or trust company). That means if you wind up putting $120,000 into a bank account and the bank fails, you will lose $20,000. So banking your entire inheritance in a traditional account is not necessarily safe. Also, the interest rates paid on these accounts are notoriously low, in the range of 1/4%."

Uncle Wayne gave me a moment to process this information and then continued. "Here's what I'd recommend. For the first little while, put 95% of the money, or more, into a high interest savings account at a major bank or financial institution. These types of accounts also qualify for the $100,000 CDIC insurance, they pay higher interest than savings and chequing accounts, and they are liquid in about three to five business days if you need the money. Also, many financial institutions have several options within them, so you can spread out the investment to achieve the $100,000 CDIC insurance, if that's important to you."

"Makes sense," I said. "I'll tell the others. Is there anything else we should do before next Saturday morning?"

Uncle Wayne said to develop what he calls a "Double O" list. We were to make a list of what we own (assets) and what we owe (liabilities), including all RRSPs, pension plans, insurance policies, money owed on credit cards, mortgages, and the like. He also suggested we gather up all our pertinent papers, including past income tax returns, plus our wills and powers of attorney. And last but not least, he suggested we make a list of our monthly income and expenditures.

By this time, we had finished our second beer, and I realized I had a lot to tell Sally, David, and Mark. I thanked Uncle Wayne, and as I motored home to get started on the floating dock, I summarized the key points so I wouldn't forget any important details:

1. Don't tell anyone about your inheritance or sudden wealth.
2. Initially put about at least 95% of the money in a high interest savings account as a cooling off period so you can think and make plans.

3. Leave just enough money to cover your regular expenses in your chequing account.

4. Make a list of what you own (RRSPs, cash, cars) and what you owe (mortgages, loans, credit cards). In addition, draw up a list of your monthly income and expenses, and gather all personal documents, such as wills, powers of attorney, mortgage documents, insurance policies, tax returns, pension plans, and other personal and financial documents.

Chapter 2

THE DOUBLE Os—WHAT YOU OWN AND WHAT YOU OWE

Even though the first meeting was set for our cottage, I was surprised when Aunt Lorraine and Mark showed up so early on Saturday morning. It seems Mark's boys had come up for the weekend with their girlfriends, and the atmosphere was a little too thick over there.

"I love my sons," Mark said, shaking his head, "but they're at that age where they're playing 'kissy-huggy' with their girlfriends all the time. Drives me crazy."

"You're just jealous because you can't get a date," I laughed. "Don't you remember what it was like to be twenty?"

"Only too well," he replied wistfully. "You know, Jack, it's very hard to meet women at my age. I've been divorced for more than a year now, and I've only had one date, and a miserable one at that."

I was waiting for the details, but just then we saw Alice and David coming down from the bunky. Alice was still friends with Mark's ex-wife, so Mark rolled his eyes and shot me one of those looks that said, "I'll talk to you later."

We had drawn straws for cooking detail that week, and Sally had lost. She doesn't cook much, making it difficult to determine who had actually lost, but she's famous for her pancake breakfasts, so we sat down at the table when Aunt Lorraine came out of the kitchen to tell us everything was ready.

We were nearly finished when we saw Uncle Wayne barreling across the bay in his Boston Whaler. My wife, Sandra, got up from the table and said she'd meet Uncle Wayne down at the dock if I would get our kids, Connor and Paige, cleaned up. They're just three and one, so getting sticky maple syrup off their little hands and faces is a bigger task than it sounds. However, I had them cleaned up and into their bathing suits in no time, so their cousins, Scott and Jan, could look after them.

Sandra and I had decided it was important for both of us to be as involved as possible in these financial meetings so that we could make decisions together about our family's future.

Aunt Lorraine thanked Sally for breakfast and went outside to say hi to Uncle Wayne before venturing home to see what Mark's boys and their girlfriends were up to.

As Scott took Connor and Paige outside, David asked if we had all made our Double-O lists of what we own and what we owe, along with a monthly accounting of our income and expenditures. We all had, except Sally. No one was particularly surprised about that.

Uncle Wayne burst into the cottage with Sandra in tow and was very direct. "It's a beautiful day, so I don't want to waste any time. Someone get me a coffee, and then let's get right to work."

I fetched the coffee, and we all gathered on the porch.

"First, let's go over your Double-O lists," Uncle Wayne said.

Sally looked a little sheepish while David pointed out that her list wasn't ready.

Uncle Wayne admonished her gently. "You've got to put some effort into this, Sally. It's very important for each of you to have a clear sense of everything you own and owe. You can't plan wisely for the future without knowing where you are today. I'd keep the Double-O list and copies of all your other financial documents in a three-ring binder and/or use a secure cloud storage service. I really like the cloud storage service, as you can access it anywhere from your computer, and all the documents are stored and backed up for you in a remote secure storage system. That makes it easy to keep track of everything, and you'll also have easy access for our meetings. I should also point out that all your original documents, such as wills, mortgage agreements, deeds to the house, and insurance policies, should be kept in a safety deposit box. If you haven't got one, get one immediately. You can also scan all of those items in a cloud storage service as well for quick access. Okay, enough lecturing. Let's go over the major liabilities that each of you have."

We could see he wasn't kidding about not wasting time. I mentioned that our major liability was the mortgage on our house. Mark had already paid off his mortgage, and David and Alice just had a small one left.

Sally said she had no liabilities at all. Uncle Wayne's eyebrows went up and his eyes got narrow. Clearly this would not be Sally's day to get off lightly.

"I hear you do a lot of shopping," he said. "Do you owe any money on your credit cards?"

"Not really," she shrugged. "I pay off the monthly minimum each time I get a bill."

Uncle Wayne just about fell out of his chair. "Sally, I don't mean to pick on you, but I can't believe what I'm hearing. You're university educated and you have a good job. Do you have any idea what kind of interest you pay on credit cards?"

David jumped in. "Are you kidding? She works for the government. What would she know about paying off debt? Those people only know how to borrow!"

Alice interrupted to save Sally. "I believe credit card interest rates are usually quite high, up to 20% depending on the card."

Uncle Wayne continued. "That's correct, Alice, and you all have debt of some type, correct?"

We all agreed.

"Do you need any of your inheritance money to live on right now?"

We all answered no, but David had an afterthought. "It depends on whether or not you think we need an emergency fund. Right now, Alice and I don't have one."

I also had wondered about an emergency fund. The advisors in the media always say to have one, but is it really necessary?

"Well," Uncle Wayne answered, "everyone should have either an emergency account or a line of credit equal to at least three months' expenses that you can get your hands on easily and quickly for emergencies, such as losing your job.[1] The best place to keep your emergency stash is in a high interest savings account.

"Once that's taken care of, the next thing you should do is pay off all your debts in this order: credit cards, personal loans, car loans, and then your mortgage."

"Why in that order?" Sally asked.

"Because the first debt to get rid of is the one with the highest interest rate, and that's usually credit cards, followed by the others I mentioned. However, there's one exception to this rule. Don't pay off loans for which the interest that is payable is deductible for tax purposes. For example, being self-employed, Mark may have some interest payments on loans that he can deduct as business expenses on his tax return, and these you would not pay off immediately."

"It's probably good advice," Alice said, "but frankly, Uncle Wayne, it's not very exciting. Wouldn't we be just as far ahead by investing a lump sum right away? At least then we could build something up."

Uncle Wayne looked at the rest of us. "Can anyone answer that question?"

Mark took a stab at it. "Well, I've been mortgage-free for a few years now, and with those payments gone, I find I have a lot of extra money every month to spend or invest."

"You have to remember," Uncle Wayne added, "that mortgage payments consist of principal and interest. When you pay off a mortgage, you wind up keeping the cash equivalent of all the interest you would

---

[1] As this book was being published, many people were being laid off due to the COVID-19 pandemic, and a three-month cash reserve would have been beneficial.

have paid over the years. You save a tremendous amount and then you can invest that money to achieve your long-term goals."

"How much could you save?" Sally asked.

I had an answer for that one. "I pulled our mortgage statement for this meeting, and when I really looked at it, I was shocked. We have a twenty-five-year mortgage for $300,000 at 3.8%. Right now, our payments are about $1,546 per month, which adds up to $18,458 per year. That sounds reasonable, but here's the kicker—after twenty-five years, we will have paid out $463,711."

Sally choked. "That's a whole lot of interest to pay!"

"Yes. By paying off the entire amount now, we'll save close to $163,711 over the long haul."

"And remember," Sandra added, "you pay a mortgage with after-tax dollars. That means at a top tax rate, Jack and I would have to put the equivalent of $36,916 earned income into our mortgage every year."

Uncle Wayne nodded. "So you see, Alice, with a 50% tax bracket, you would have to find an investment that will pay a guaranteed rate of return equal to 7.6% just to stay even if you're also making mortgage payments at 3.8%. In effect, paying off a mortgage is a guaranteed investment."

David was worried that early pay-off penalties would be costly, but Uncle Wayne assured him that the future savings may be well worth the penalty charged by financial institutions. He would have to confirm what the actual charges were, and he'd have to "do the math."

Uncle Wayne then explained the advantage of paying a mortgage bi-weekly versus monthly. "If you pay your mortgage bi-weekly on an accelerated basis, your mortgage will be paid off in twenty-two years versus twenty-five years, and this saves a lot of interest."

Mark added, "I'm mortgage-free, and it sure is a good feeling."

Right about then, David and Alice's kids came in and asked when Uncle Jack could take them water-skiing. I guess they were tired of babysitting. I can't recall exactly when I became the designated boat driver for these things, but it had been that way for years.

Uncle Wayne said I could take them now. "We're finished for today."

"What about next week?" Sally asked.

Uncle Wayne laughed. "Now that you're all going to follow my excellent advice and pay off your debts, I want you to redo your Double-O lists. Then I want you to consider seriously which of these three main goals you want your inheritance to achieve:

1. Do you need the cash now to pay off debts or for purchases? (liquidity)
2. Do you need to set up an income plan from the inheritance to fund your current expenses and lifestyle?
3. Is the inheritance earmarked to provide for your future retirement income?

"Decide individually what your priorities are relative to your personal and career objectives, and then we can devise specific strategies for each of you to handle your inheritance."

Sandra walked Uncle Wayne down to the dock and helped push off his boat. As I went up to the shed to grab the water skis and rope, I began to summarize in my mind the main points we would be discussing together this week:

1. Put a complete list of everything you owe and own and copies of all legal and financial documents in a three-ring binder for easy reference, and/or utilize a secure cloud service. Originals of the documents should be in a safety deposit box.
2. Establish an easily accessible emergency fund equal to three months' expenses, or obtain a line of credit.
3. Pay off all debts that aren't deductible for income tax purposes and do it in the order of highest interest rates, which is credit cards first and then loans and mortgages.
4. Pay off what you owe to generate the highest guaranteed return on your investment and increase your cash flow.
5. Decide relative priorities for the three main goals your inheritance could achieve: cash for today, current income, or for your future retirement.

Chapter 3

PROTECTING AND PRESERVING YOUR WEALTH

"Well, David, I have to say one thing—you sure have become a good cook. This has been one of the best breakfasts we've had all summer."

David's face was rife with suspicion as he glanced over at Alice. "It's only our second Saturday breakfast, dear, and I think I know why you're buttering me up. You just want me to take over cooking detail during the week too. Nice try, but no deal."

"If you think this is impressive, wait until you see what I've got in store for you when you come over to our place next weekend," Mark bragged.

"Aunt Lorraine, can you do the cooking next week?" Sally pleaded. "Mark has never made anything even remotely edible, and you know how much we all love your crepes."

Aunt Lorraine got up from the table and said, "David, thank you for breakfast. As for the rest of you, I think you'll be surprised when you see Mark in action next Saturday. These days women want a man who can take care of himself, so I've been teaching him how to find his way around a kitchen."

After Aunt Lorraine left, I asked everyone whether they had followed any of Uncle Wayne's advice during the past week by starting to pay off their debts.

"I have," Sally answered. "I paid off all my credit cards, and I'm going to pay the total every month now instead of just the minimum, so I won't be charged any interest."

"Atta girl, Sal. You've learned something already," Mark said.

"Mark, I don't much care for the condescending tone in your voice," she countered, "and you had better quit referring to women my age as 'girls.' It would appear that the politically correct parade has passed you by. No wonder you can't get a date!"

"I, for one, don't want to hear about Mark's social life," Alice said. "Getting back to Jack's question, our mortgage is coming up for renewal in about two months, so we're going to do what makes the most financial sense. We'll apply our double-up payments and the anniversary payment now and then pay off the balance at renewal time."

"I've never had a mortgage," Sally said, "so you just lost me, Alice. What are double-up and anniversary payments?"

"Well," she answered, "there are lots of different kinds of mortgages, but I did some checking, and ours lets us pay an amount equivalent to the monthly mortgage payment, in addition to our regular payment, each month. That's the double-up feature. The extra payment is applied directly against the principal, which is the amount that was borrowed in the first place."

"And that would mean the interest component on the remaining mortgage payments would be less," Sally reasoned, "because you've made a deeper dent in the principal."

"Bingo."

"Do all mortgages have this double-up feature?" Sally asked.

"No, they don't," Alice replied. "You have to check the terms and conditions of each particular mortgage."

"Wait a minute," Mark interrupted, "I thought extra payments like that were only allowed on the anniversary date of the mortgage … you know, when the day rolls around every year that you first signed the papers."

"Well, that might have been true for your mortgage, but not ours," Alice explained. "Ours was a closed mortgage, and besides the double-up feature, ours allows a one-time 10% at any time during the year, and it's applied directly against the principal. By the way, the reason we aren't paying off the entire mortgage now is that we wouldn't save a dime. In fact, the penalty payments for an early pay-off would be more than the interest we'll be paying over the next two months until we're up for renewal."

I smiled at Alice with respect and set out to explain the mortgage situation for Sandra and me.

"First, we took advantage of the terms of our mortgage by making an anniversary payment, much like yours, Alice. Then we arranged to pay off the remainder of our mortgage, with a penalty, at the end of this month. Come to think of it, it's a good thing we'd put our cash in a high interest savings account, because Sandra was able to get at the money in a matter of two days."

"Daddy, Daddy, boat, Uncle Wayne," Connor was pointing toward the dock as we saw Uncle Wayne bounce over in his Boston Whaler.

As bright as our kids are, they weren't ready for a discussion about investment strategy, so once again Connor and Paige were put in the care of Scott and Jan so that the adults could concentrate on the business at hand.

Uncle Wayne came in the door, grabbed a coffee, and immediately started talking.

INVESTMENT STRATEGIES TO PROTECT YOUR INHERITANCE

"I hope you've perfected your golf swings, because the annual Honey Harbour Tournament is next Saturday, and I have entered all of us.

"Meanwhile, here's my plan for today's session. First, we'll talk about the types of investments that can help each of you achieve your financial objectives. Then we'll focus on protecting your inheritance, and, finally, we'll look at tax and retirement planning."

"I have to admit that I'm really getting a kick out of these sessions," Alice grinned. "I'm actually more interested in this stuff than David, and I've been doing a fair bit of research.

"You wanted us to think about priorities for the three main objectives we could achieve with our inheritance, which are:

1. Do you need the cash now to pay off debts or for purchases? (liquidity)
2. Do you need to set up an income plan from the inheritance to fund your current expenses and lifestyle?
3. Is the inheritance earmarked to provide for your future retirement income?

"Of course, priorities depend largely on age and situation. As you all know, David and I are both in our early fifties. Soon we'll be paying off the small mortgage we still have on our house with David's inheritance. We've established an emergency fund equal to three months' expenses, and we've also decided to set aside enough to cover university for the kids.

"David plans to continue working in the equipment leasing business, where he gets both a salary and a bonus. I've been teaching since Scott and Jan started high school.

"Still, we don't need the inheritance to provide an income for us at this point. Our main goal is growth, because we're looking to retire in about five to ten years if possible. Those are the facts, Uncle Wayne. How do you think we should invest our money?"

"Let's hear from the others before we get into individual plans," he answered. "What's up with you, Sally?"

"Well, I have no immediate need for cash for a large purchase, but I'll probably want to buy a house someday. I'm just not sure when. My job situation depends a lot on cutbacks and the federal deficit. I'd always thought I'd stay in Ottawa and work for the government until I retired, but I'm only thirty-five, so that's at least another twenty-five to thirty years away. I guess these days most people can't count on being with one employer for their entire working lives. Anyway, that's about as far ahead as I've been able to look."

Sandra followed Sally and told everyone that she would continue to work part-time as a teacher until both Connor and Paige were in school all day. We were comfortable with our earned income, so we didn't need the income our inheritance could produce for living expenses. Since we're both forty, we were hoping to retire in twenty years, or twenty-five at most.

Mark said his software business in Kitchener was doing well, and he was looking to retire in the next year or two, as he is sixty-three. He also mentioned that his divorce was almost final, and he was thinking of buying a smaller house. His two sons were away at university completing their master's degrees, and he neither expected nor particularly wanted them to move back home on a full-time basis.

Alice had listened politely but was clearly getting impatient. "So, Uncle Wayne, you know our situations. What should we invest in?"

"For starters," replied Uncle Wayne, "let's look at the three investment classes— cash, bonds, and equities/stocks—and review what you'd be getting into with each."

"I'd like to take a stab at this," declared Mark. "In the first two categories, cash and bonds, you're basically lending money to another party, but with stocks, you're buying shares, or ownership, in a company. Over the long term, stocks have outperformed the other types of investments."

"Details!" demanded Sally. "More details, please."

"Sure. In the category of cash, you've got savings and chequing accounts, and Treasury Bills (T-Bills). T-Bills are sold every Tuesday by the Government of Canada, for terms from thirty days up to a year. They're sold at a discount, which means they're sold at less than their face value, but at the maturity date, you get the full face value; therefore, the deeper the discount, the better return you'll get. I also found out that the reason the government issues T-Bills is that it provides them with a way to raise cash."

"Maybe I was wrong about you, Mark. Maybe you do know something after all," Alice said with a grin from ear to ear. "Now tell us about bonds."

"I'll take that as a compliment, I think," said Mark. "When you buy bonds, you're really making a loan, either to a level of government, which could be federal, provincial, or municipal, or to a company. They, in turn, promise to pay you a set interest rate for a certain period of time, and when that time's up, they pay back your loan."

"Wait a minute, hotshot," Alice said. "What about GICs? Are they considered cash or bonds?" She was a sly one.

Uncle Wayne jumped in to save Mark. "I would include GICs in the bond category, because they have some of the same characteristics as bonds."

"That's what I was about to say," Mark declared, although he looked as though he didn't expect us to believe him. "Anyway, GIC stands for Guaranteed Investment Certificate, and, essentially, it's a loan you give to a bank or trust company. The usual term for a GIC is one to five years, although it can be longer. For example, you loan the bank $1,000, and the bank will pay you a set interest rate for a specific period of time and then pay back your $1,000. A lot of people like GICs because they're guaranteed for up to $100,000 per institution per person by the Canada Deposit Insurance Corporation (CDIC), provided that the term of the GIC doesn't exceed five years."

"So what's the difference between a bond and a GIC?" asked Sally.

"There are two main differences: the guarantee factor and the liquidity. You usually can't cash in a GIC before the end of the set term. A bond has more liquidity; you can sell it on the open market anytime you want. However, the value of the bond is not guaranteed. If you sell it before the maturity date, you could end up losing money, or if you're lucky, making money."

"You'll have to run that by me again," Sally complained. "You're starting to lose me."

"No problem, cousin. What's probably confusing you is my use of the word 'value.' You see, a bond's value is not the price you paid for it but something that is determined by the current interest rates. For example, if you bought a $1,000 bond that paid an interest rate, also called a coupon rate, of 3% per year, you would receive $30 a year in interest, and if you held on to the bond until its maturity date, you'd get back your $1,000. But if you needed cash in a hurry and sold your bond before the maturity date, the value of the bond would be determined by current interest rates at the time of the sale.

"For example, if interest rates had risen to 5% since the time you bought the bond, no one is going to pay you the full $1,000, because your bond only pays 3% interest, and the buyer could get 5% by investing somewhere else. So to sell your bond, you have to drop the price so that the buyer gets the equivalent of a 5% return on the investment."

"So bonds are more liquid than GICs," Sally summarized, "but if you sell them before maturity, the value will vary according to current interest rates."

"That explains a lot," Alice said. "I'd read you could post a capital gain or loss with bonds, and now I know how."

"When you buy stocks," Mark continued, "you're not lending money to the company; you're actually buying ownership in a company. Your investment increases when the value of the company increases; unfortunately, it also works the opposite way. If the value of the company decreases, so does your investment. Some companies also pay their investors a portion of the company profits each year in the form of dividends. Dividends are nice, but your biggest gain comes when the value of the company goes up, because that pushes up the value of your stocks."

"I'll say it again," interrupted Alice. "I'm impressed, and I don't impress easily."

"Tell me about it," mused David.

The rest of us laughed, but Sally had dollar signs in her eyes. "Are stocks guaranteed?"

"No way!" Mark answered.

"Well then, why would anyone buy them?"

Uncle Wayne took over. "It's true that the stock market goes up and down, but over the long term, the trend has been up, just like the economy. I can show this to you in black and white. I took the liberty of asking Aunt Lorraine what year each of you were born so that I could chart the growth of the Toronto Stock Exchange Index in a way that isn't skewed toward my point of view. Look at this," he said as he pulled out a sheet of paper.

Mark	(1955)	TSE was 536.50
David	(1968)	TSE was 1062.88
Alice	(1970)	TSE was 947.54
Jack/Sandra	(1978)	TSE was 1309.99
Sally	(1983)	TSE was 2552.35

"The Toronto Stock Exchange at the end of 2019 was at a whopping 17,063.43, so even with all the turbulence in the time since Mark was born, the stock market has increased dramatically. Gosh, think of everything that has happened in the last sixty-three years: the Korean War, the Cuban missile crisis, Vietnam, the separatist movement in Quebec, the advent of the information society and the global economy, not to mention the oil crisis of 1973, the market crash of '87, the fall of Communism, the Gulf Wars, Bre-X, Nortel, the Dot Com boom bust in 2000–2001, the Great Recession in 2008–2009, 9/11 ..."

"Enough with the history," Sandra said affectionately. "Let's get back to the economy. What I think you're saying is that at any one point in time, there's enough upheaval going on that you could feel skittish about risking an investment in stocks. However, the bottom line is that the market has always gone up over the long term."

"I'm still not crazy about the risk factor," Sally said. "Stocks may have gone up over time, but how have cash and bond investments done in comparison?"

"I thought someone might ask that," Uncle Wayne replied, "so I came prepared. The information for this chart came from the 2018 Morningstar Andex Chart, and it shows the average performance of each over various time periods."

Last Ten Years

Asset	Compounded Annual Return	Risk
T-bills (91 days)	0.9%	4.1%
5 Year GICs	1.8%	3.6%
US Large Stocks	13.0%	17.0%
World Stocks	6.4%	20.1%
Canadian Stocks	4.2%	16.5%
Long Bonds	6.7%	9.6%
Balanced Portfolio	7.5%	10.0%
CPI (Inflation)	1.5%	

Last Twenty Years

Asset	Compounded Annual Return	Risk
T-bills (91 days)	2.3%	4.1%
5 Year GICs	2.7%	3.6%
US Large Stocks	5.9%	17.0%
World Stocks	4.3%	20.1%
Canadian Stocks	6.6%	16.5%
Long Bonds	6.8%	9.6%
Balanced Portfolio	6.4%	10.0%
CPI (Inflation)	1.9%	

Since 1950

Asset	Compounded Annual Return	Risk
T-bills (91 days)	5.2 %	4.1%
5 Year GICs	6.2%	3.6%
US Large Stocks	11.7%	17.0%
Canadian Stocks	9.8%	16.5%
Long Bonds	7.4%	9.6%
Balanced Portfolio	9.5%	10.0%
CPI (Inflation)	3.6%	

"What the heck does the risk percentage mean?" I asked as I studied my copy.

"Good question," said our uncle, turning toward me. "Look at the last twenty years; the average return for Canadian stocks was 6.6%. The risk figure is 16.5 percentage points, which means that the returns in any one year could have been as high as 26.3%, or as low as -9.9%. The fluctuation figure tells us the extent of the range for returns on stocks."

"I'm still not clear on this," I admitted.

"Try thinking of it in terms of your golf score, Jack. On average, you shoot about 110 for eighteen holes, but your range is probably anywhere from about 102 to 118."

"Hey, what about the time I shot 95?" I protested.

"That's a good point," Uncle Wayne agreed. "Sometimes a result will be well outside of the range, but as you know from your golf game, that happens very rarely."

"I see," Sally said. "The fluctuation is the standard deviation, which means that the result will be within the range two times out of three. However, there is always a possibility that a result will be outside the boundaries of the range, like what happened in 2008."

We all stared at Sally.

"No big deal," she shrugged. "Stats 101."

"So," I commented, "if the results will be within the range of fluctuation two out of three times, then investing in the stocks of good companies would be the best investment over the long term. However, since the result could be outside the range one out of three times, and that means higher or lower, you have to be emotionally and financially prepared to handle the risk factor."

"I understand this," Sally said, "but I don't want the headaches of worrying about ups and downs. I'm going to sink all of my money into bonds and GICs, and I'll be fine."

"Not so fast, Sally," said Uncle Wayne. "You haven't considered the other risk factors related to investment planning, namely inflation, taxes, and the very real worry that you might outlive your supply of money."

Again, Uncle Wayne shuffled through his papers to fish out another chart for us.

"Let's say that in 2019, you invested $100,000 for a twenty-year period in a GIC with an average return of 3.5% before taxes:

2019 $100,000 (investment)
2038 $198,979 (3.5% return, no taxes)

"But you do have to pay taxes, so let's assume your tax rate is 40%. That would mean your after tax growth is 2.1%, so let's add that factor to the list.

2019 $100,000 (investment)
2038 $198,797 (3.5% return, no taxes)
2038 $151,536 (2.1% return, after tax)

"Your investment doesn't look so healthy anymore, and we're not even finished. We must count inflation as another factor, so let's use a long-term inflation average of 2% and add that to our list.

2019 $100,000 (investment)
2038 $198,797 (3.5% return, no taxes)
2038 $151,536 (2.1% return, after tax)
2038 $101,979 (0.1% return, after tax, after inflation of 2%)

"What looked like a good investment before taxes and inflation now appears to be pretty darn poor. Your $100,000 has only grown to $101,979 in today's dollars after twenty long years."

"Are you saying I should invest everything in stocks?" Sally asked.

"I don't think that would be within your comfort zone, Sally," he answered. "Could you stand seeing your entire portfolio down by 50% in any one year, like 2008, if you invested only in US stocks?"

"Hardly," she replied. "I think I'd flip right out."

"Then perhaps the answer, for all of you, is something called 'asset allocation.' Essentially it means not putting all your eggs in one basket.

"Several studies have shown that the most important factor in determining the success of investments is asset allocation. I won't bore you with all the findings, but the highlights are:

1. the allocation between stocks, bonds, and cash can account for up to 85% to 95% of the difference in returns between various portfolios; and
2. different asset allocations represent different risk levels but may end up providing the same level of returns. The key is to figure out which mix will bring the returns you want while offering the lowest possible risk."

As we tried to absorb this information, Uncle Wayne looked at us thoughtfully and continued.

"The money you've received has come by way of your parents' hard work and sound planning. I believe it should not be gambled with, and you should try to protect the capital as much as possible. However, since you'll want to provide for your own retirement as well as leave some money behind for your children, you're going to need some growth too.

"My best advice is to develop a globally diversified portfolio that invests both in bonds and stocks/equities, based on your risk level and specific goals."

"What kind of mix do you recommend?" asked Alice.

"Before we get into that, Alice, let's review what I mean by risk," Uncle Wayne continued as he sat up straight in his chair. "There are basically two main types of risk: capital preservation risk and inflation risk.

"Capital preservation risk is the risk that your capital is not there when you need it. Let's say you were going to buy a new boat in a year, and the cost was $25,000. To make sure you had the $25,000 in a year, you would have to invest in conservative investments, such as a high interest savings account, so you'd have the $25,000. If you invested in equities/stocks, in a year you could have more than $25,000 or a lot less.

"Inflation risk is basically making sure that your money grows over time as items get more expensive each year. Even inflation of 2% over twenty years, as in the prior example, can lead to costs increasing dramatically.

"Even if you're close to retirement, you still need some growth in your portfolio, because people today are living longer, and the longer you live, the greater the chance is that inflation will beat you. I'm sure you all want to live a long time, but you don't want to outlive your supply of money, so your financial plans should be based on a projected lifespan to your mid-nineties. That means Sally needs her money for the next sixty years, and Mark for another forty-two!"

Mark looked surprised and took a sip of his drink. "Wow, that is a long time. I wonder if I'll still be water skiing then!"

Sally started to laugh and said, "You can barely water ski now! You only go once a year after a few brown pops!"

Uncle Wayne coughed to get our attention and continued. "So you all will need growth or equites in your portfolio to keep up with inflation. A globally diversified portfolio is made up of both bonds and stocks/equities from countries around the world, and the breakdown is determined by both your goals and your risk, or sleep at night factor."

"What specifically do you mean by goals and sleep at night factor?" asked Sally.

"Let me try to answer that," Alice went on. "For short term goals, say when you will need the money in less than five years, you'll want to use conservative or defensive investments like short term-bonds, GICs, or high interest savings accounts, so that the money is there when you need it.

"Longer term goals can be more difficult to plan for. For example, if you can attain your retirement income goals based on only investing in GICs and/or bonds, then the risk of your portfolio will be low, and it will not fluctuate much. Since your money growth is more consistent, you're better able to sleep at night, because you really don't need to worry too much about your portfolio declining in value.

"However, for many people, us included, to achieve our retirement income goals, we need higher returns than what bonds or GICs can provide ... so we must invest in stocks. This is where the sleep at night factor comes in. The greater the allocation to stocks or equities, the greater the fluctuation—daily, monthly, and annually—of the portfolio returns and portfolio. This fluctuation of returns is called your risk level, or sleep at night factor. If you can't sleep at night because your portfolio value changes too much, you may need more capital preservation type of investments in your portfolio; however, if you do this, you may not generate the returns required to achieve your goals. So how did I do, Uncle Wayne?"

"Awesome, Alice, I couldn't have said it any better!"

"So how do you actually develop a diversified portfolio?" asked Sally. "I understand the basics between bonds and equities, and clearly I haven't been doing as much research and reading as Alice. How do we put it all together?"

"From my experience," Uncle Wayne continued, "there are six key factors to developing a globally diversified portfolio, and they are:

1. strategic asset allocation
2. tactical asset allocation
3. specific investments and/or money managers
4. risk management
5. fees
6. taxes

"Whole books have been written about this subject; however, I will attempt to simplify this. Strategic asset allocation is basically what we have reviewed, and it's your long-term allocation between bonds and equities. This also includes how much you would invest in Canada, the US, and internationally for both bonds and stocks."

Alice commented, "Is one of the reasons that we should invest outside of Canada because different countries' economies and companies do well at different times, so by investing outside of Canada, we can reduce our risk?"

"Yup, that's it," Uncle Wayne said with a smile.

"So then tactical asset allocation," Sally added, "would be shorter term allocation changes based on market conditions?"

"Correct," continued Uncle Wayne. "It could be a decision to increase your allocation slightly to Canadian equities or increase an allocation to international bonds."

"I've been doing some reading," I mentioned. "So for the actual investments, we could pick the stocks or bonds ourselves or use mutual funds, exchange-traded funds (ETFs), index funds, and/or use a managed money approach using a professional portfolio manager. I've been wondering, though. What are ETFs and index funds exactly?"

"Well," Uncle Wayne continued, "ETFs are similar to mutual funds in that they can be a basket of securities, such as stocks and bonds; however, they're traded directly on a stock exchange, which means they're bought and sold like stock. Many track the performance of a specific stock market index and/or asset class. These are often referred to as index funds. For example, at the most basic level, you can buy an ETF or index fund that follows the performance of the Toronto Stock Exchange (TSX), so you would get exposure to all the companies in the TSX. Today, some ETFs are wrapped in a mutual fund as well. It can get very confusing, and as a result it can be difficult and/or time consuming to select and monitor your own investments over time, but we'll talk about that in a minute.

"Let's finish the last three factors first. I had mentioned risk management, and these are techniques that professional money managers use to reduce the risk of a portfolio. An example would be to use a currency hedge to protect returns. When you invest outside of Canada, your investment is valued normally in the home country's currency. To protect your investment from dramatic swings in the currency of another country versus the Canadian dollar, professional money managers can use a hedging strategy."

"Is this used because our portfolio is valued in Canadian Dollars, and investments outside of Canada are converted back to Canadian Dollars?" asked Mark.

"Bingo!" Uncle Wayne continued. "After risk management, another factor is fees. These would be the fees you would pay your financial advisor for their advice, and the fees for the investments themselves. Like all things in life, you must get value for the fees you pay. You could invest yourself and save on the fees, or you could hire a professional. It really depends on what you're looking for and your own money management expertise.

"The last key factor is taxation. You'll want your investments to be held in a tax effective manner, and you also want to organize your investments in a way to reduce the amount of taxes you have to pay."

"This is a lot of stuff to know," said Mark. "I'm glad we have you to help us!"

"While I can provide good general overview, you either must hire an advisor yourself, or really do a lot of reading and research. Jack asked about what type of investments to select. I recommend the use of a globally diversified portfolio, and I'd suggest using a professional money manager using a portfolio approach. The specific investments could be individual stocks and bonds, mutual funds, ETFs, index funds, or a combination of them all." As he spoke, he handed out a piece of paper.

"The type of portfolio allocations will be specific to each of you based on your goal requirements, time frames, and risk level. I looked at the basic portfolios from Morningstar, which is what my CFP®, or CERTIFIED FINANCIAL PLANNER®, professional uses when updating my financial plan, and these are the base portfolios' projected returns and risk levels."

Portfolio Type	Defensive	Growth	Projected Returns	Risk
Conservative	80 %	20%	3.60%	4.27%
Moderate Conservative	60%	40%	4.23%	5.42%
Moderate	40%	60%	4.90%	7.34%
Moderate Aggressive	25%	75%	5.35%	9.01%
Aggressive	10%	90%	5.82%	10.70%

Source: Morningstar November 2019
Defensive=income investments, Growth=stock/equity investments

"So," Sally said as she took a drink and paused, "let me see if I understand this. If we look at the moderate portfolio, the 40% defensive means that the allocation would be 40% income type of investments like bonds, and the 60% growth means that it has 60 % equity investments, with a long-term projected return of 4.90%. Also, the risk level of 7.34%, would be the range of returns. Is that correct, Uncle Wayne?"

"Absolutely!" Uncle Wayne said with pride. "What your financial advisor should do is review your plan based on your risk level, and if you can't achieve your goals, one option would be to increase the potential returns, and that might mean moving from the moderate portfolio to the moderate aggressive portfolio for some of your investments."

Sally asked another question. "Why are the returns for the portfolios less than the returns you showed us over the past number of years?"

Uncle Wayne took a sip of his drink and then replied. "The main reason is that they look at the current market conditions and make a forecast going forward. This is updated every year or so to keep current. The secondary reason is that if you use projections that are too high, it makes your plan unrealistic."

"That makes sense, Uncle Wayne," continued Mark. "I'm looking at retiring. Does this change my investment strategy at all?" He got up and grabbed another drink.

WHAT ABOUT RETIREMENT INCOME AND CASH-FLOW PLANNING?

"The key thing is that once you retire, you'll want to create a strategy to replace the monthly paycheque you've been receiving for the past thirty to forty years with the assets you've accumulated over your lifetime. The basics still apply; however, there is a slight change in approach. Do you remember when you were younger and we used to go to Blueberry Hill, climb up the rock cliff, pick the blueberries, and then climb down? Later, you took your own kids."

"Absolutely, but why do you mentioned that?"

"When you took your own kids, did you let them go ahead of you on the way up to the top of the rock cliff?"

"Yes, we did."

"And then on the way down, were they allowed to go alone?" asked Uncle Wayne.

"No, we used to hold their little hands when climbing down," Mark continued.

"Why was that?" asked Uncle Wayne

"Well, on the way up, if they slipped or fell, they'd just fall down a bit, and we were there to pick them up and start again. On the way down, if they slipped or fell, they could tumble to the bottom and really get hurt," Mark explained.

"This sort of explains the difference between saving for retirement and retiring with the need to generate an income and cash-flow stream from the assets you have accumulated and inherited. The way up the rock cliff is like saving for retirement. If you make a small mistake or slip, you can recover and continue your journey to the top. However, once you reach the top and start the descent, it's like being retired. If you make a mistake, you have less time to recover. You could tumble to the bottom and get hurt badly.

"Just like when you held your kids' hands on the way down the rock cliff to protect them, an experienced retirement income advisor can help retirees navigate their income and cash-flow requirements."

"That's a great analogy, Uncle Wayne. I can see how it's important to make sure you have a great plan as you transition to retirement, but what are some of the key risks to retirement income planning that are different than saving for retirement?" Mark asked.

RISKS TO RETIREMENT INCOME PLANNING

"Good question, Mark. A key risk is that you really don't know how long you must plan for, which is called longevity risk. People are living longer today and don't want to out-live their investments," Uncle Wayne explained.

"I was reading some stats the other day, and for a couple today at age sixty-five, there's a 50% chance one will live to ninety, and a 25% chance that one will live to ninety-five," I added.

"Wow," Sally said. "Mark, if you ever get a new girlfriend, you'll have to plan for another thirty-three years!"

"Good luck with that," Alice commented with a smirk on her face.

"Let's get back on track. We've already reviewed inflation risk and taxation risk over time, so another key risk we must review is something called sequence of return risk," Uncle Wayne said.

"What in the world does that mean?" Sandra asked.

"I've been doing some reading, and I believe it means that in retirement or just prior to retirement, if you have poor investment returns, it can dramatically reduce your long-term income," Mark suggested.

Uncle Wayne continued. "You are correct, but I want to add to that. When saving for retirement, if you average 4.90% with a moderate portfolio over ten years, we know that you don't actually have a return of 4.90% every single year. You could have years when you get higher than 4.90% and years when the returns could be negative. When saving for retirement, you can take advantage of down years by adding more money to your savings. The challenge is that once you stop working, and you're taking money out of your investments every year, if you have bad early years in retirement, it can reduce your investment account balance, and you don't have time to make it up. As a result, your retirement income can be determined by luck, which can be either good or bad, depending on when you start withdrawals."

"Ouch," commented Alice. "So that means two people could have the exact same investments and retire seven to eight years apart and have completely different experiences and retirement incomes. Are there any other risks we need to review?"

"Yes, there are few. One is cognitive risk, which means as people age, they may not be able to make financial and health decisions for themselves. We'll review powers of attorney in a later session. Another risk that I worry about for myself is health risk, which refers to staying healthy as I get older, and the real worry that one day I may have to move into a retirement home and then perhaps a long-term care facility," Uncle Wayne suggested.

"You still look pretty healthy to us," Sally added. "I bet you can still water ski better than Mark!"

"I'm sure he can," Mark added. "You've been retired for a while. How much income do we actually need in retirement, Uncle Wayne?"

HOW MUCH INCOME DO YOU NEED IN RETIREMENT?

Uncle Wayne got up, walked to the counter, and poured another glass of orange juice. "I like to break it down into day-to-day expenses, which are your normal daily living expenses and what I call 'do what you want when you want' spending, which is really your fun money. This could be travel, bird watching, writing a novel, and perhaps your bucket list items. For this spending, I'd suggest you plan to do that in your first ten to fifteen years of retirement, when you're healthy.

"Other costs to consider would be replacement costs for things such as a new roof, furnace, or car. Also, you have contingencies that may occur, such as helping grandkids with their education, or health care expenses, such as funds for a retirement home or a long-term care facility, or extra help at home if required."

"That's a lot of stuff to think of," Mark commented. "Where do we start?"

"I'd suggest the starting point is to determine how much you want to spend each year, so look at your current expenses and then deduct what expenses you may no longer have once you stop working. Next, determine your sources of guaranteed income, such as Old Age Security, Canada Pension Plan, and company pension plans like Sally has. The difference between your guaranteed sources of income and what you want to spend is how much income or cash flow you'll require from your own investments. Once you find this out, you can see if conservative investments such as GICs or bonds will provide you the income you require for the rest of your lives. If not, you'll have to look at other options." Uncle Wayne sorted through his papers and gave each of us a sheet. "I had thought that you might ask this question, Mark, as you've hinted at retiring over the last several months, so I printed this out yesterday for you to review."

"The Wayner is always thinking ahead," I added.

RETIREMENT INCOME PLANNING OPTIONS

"There are five main options to achieve the cash flow you desire from your own assets:

1. income only investing
2. income focused investing
3. guaranteed income: life income annuity/guaranteed income products
4. total return investing: diversified portfolio
5. combination of the above.

"Let's start with income only investing first," Uncle Wayne continued. "With this option, you would only invest in bonds or GICs, and the income they provide is what you use for spending. This is often the starting point in creating a retirement income and cash-flow plan. The challenge with this approach is that with the current low yield environment, the income earned may not be enough to fund your cash flow needs annually. Over time, the asset growth may not allow you to keep up with inflation, as your cash flow needs increase."

"So," Alice asked, "low yield means low interest rates, and with the current interest rates so low, it could be difficult to create the income from the money you invest? We couldn't really increase our income each year in retirement, sort of like when we received a raise while working?"

"You got it, Alice."

"What about the second option? How is income focused investing different from interest only investing?" Alice continued.

"With income focused investing," Uncle Wayne said, "not only would you invest in income-oriented investments such as GICs and bonds, but you'd also invest in dividend paying stocks, either directly or within mutual funds, and live off the income they provide.

"As with the income only investing, the challenge with this approach is that with the current low yield and interest rates, as Alice mentioned, the income and dividends earned may not be enough to fund your income and cash flow needs. Over time, the asset growth may not allow you to keep up with inflation as your cash flow needs increase."

"That makes sense to me," David commented. "Next on the list is annuities. I've heard about them, but how exactly do annuities work?"

"Well," Uncle Wayne started, "a life annuity isn't really an investment but a tool to create income. It's like purchasing your own pension. With this option, you would purchase an annuity from a life insurance company and then receive a guaranteed income for life, or for joint life with your spouse or partner. Annuities can be purchased with registered investments (RRSPs and RRIFs), and the income is fully taxable each year. Annuities purchased with non-registered funds may have a tax advantage.

"A key advantage of annuities is that they eliminate the risk of out-living your savings and market risks, which are transferred to the life insurance company."

Sandra commented, "I take it to mean that with life annuities, as long as you're alive, you'll get paid, so that takes care of outliving your savings."

"And when you say market risk, Uncle Wayne, I assume you're referring to when the markets have terrible years, like 2008," said Alice. "What happens to your capital when you purchase an annuity?"

"Both of you are correct, Alice. As long as you're alive, you'll receive your income, and market risk is exactly what happened in 2008. An advantage to annuities is that once purchased, no more decisions are made. However, the trade-off is that for the lifetime guaranteed income, you no longer have access to your capital. Some life insurance companies do offer cash back annuities, which means that at death, if payments you received haven't equalled the original purchase price of the annuity, the difference goes to your estate."

"So if you don't have a pension like me, Jack could buy an annuity and sort of replicate a pension for lifetime income?" asked Sandra.

"Absolutely," grinned Uncle Wayne. "Some people don't like the thought of using their capital to purchase an annuity, so another option for guaranteed income is guaranteed income products offered by life insurance companies through their segregated funds, which are pooled investments like mutual funds. These products provide a lifetime guarantee of income regardless of how the underlying investments perform within the segregated fund contract.

"Most often the guaranteed income will be less than what an annuity would provide; however, you do have full access to your capital at any time at the current market value. If you do redeem your money, you no longer have the income guarantees. These products are flexible enough that if your needs change, you can get your money back. I have friends who retired prior to the 2008/2009 financial crash, and they found these types of income products to be very helpful in providing guaranteed income for part of their income and cash-flow strategy."[2]

"Sounds complicated," I added, "but I can see that having some guaranteed income in retirement on top of Canada Pension Plan and Old Age Security would help with the sleep at night factor."

Mark added, "I've been talking to some of my friends who have already retired, and to a person they've said that those who have more guaranteed income worry less about their own investment portfolios. So how does the next option work, investing using a globally diversified portfolio?"

"This approach is like what you would do prior to retirement," Uncle Wayne explained. "You'd invest in a globally diversified portfolio that will generate income, dividends, and capital gains, so that you don't totally rely on only one source of income. The inclusion of capital gains allows you the potential of keeping up with inflation over time. This is called a total return portfolio.

"To create a monthly income, like your paycheque when working, you withdraw the cash flow you require. The withdrawal amount can be changed to adjust for an increase or decrease in your retirement expenses. For example, during the Great Recession (December 2007 to June 2009), I reduced my 'do what I want, when I want' spending that year until the markets rebounded the following years. With a total return portfolio, many retirees may end up with an asset allocation in the range of between 40% to 60% growth investments, and 60% to 40% defensive investments.

"Often with this strategy, a 'bucket' approach is used, where the first two to three years of spending is placed in the 'income bucket' and allocated to very conservative investments, such as a high interest

---

[2]   These products are designed to protect a retiree's income and cash-flow from financial market declines, like during the COVID-19 Pandemic.

savings account or short-term bonds, and the cash flow is redeemed from this location first. The balance is allocated to the longer-term portfolio, the diversified portfolio bucket. At the end of each year, the income bucket is filled up from the diversified portfolio bucket if the market growth has been positive."

"I think this would help with sequence of return risk. Is that correct, Uncle Wayne?" asked Alice.

"Absolutely," Uncle Wayne answered.

"This all sounds very complicated," Mark commented. "How do you review the various tax strategies?"

"First of all, you need a great accountant and CFP, and there are some great financial planning software packages that good financial planners can use to model the different options."

Uncle Wayne then added, "Many retirees like me will develop a plan where they may utilize a combination of the above options to create their lifelong income and cash-flow plan. For example, retirees may decide to cover some of their essential expenses with an annuity or a guaranteed income product and then invest the balance in a total return portfolio, perhaps using a bucketing approach.

"A key part of this approach is the coordination from a timing, sequencing, and tax standpoint, as retirees may have numerous income sources, such as:

- Old Age Security and Canada Pension Plan;
- company pension plans;
- RRSPs, RRIFs, locked in RRSPs;
- tax free savings accounts (TFSAs);
- annuities and guaranteed income products; and
- non-registered investment accounts.

"So there's a great need to develop an optimal de-accumulation strategy, and this is where a great financial planner can help."

"Awesome stuff, Wayner, as Jack would say," commented Mark. "This helps to explain the analogy of the difference between climbing up Blueberry Hill and climbing down. I can see that once you retire, decisions become more difficult and important."

"I don't think I can remember all this, Uncle Wayne," Sandra said, sounding a bit perplexed. "I can see why we need a good accountant and financial planner for the times when we can't get hold of you."

"You bet. Remember, I am away most of the winter. In one of our later sessions, we'll talk about building your own team of financial advisors," he replied. "But as long as you have a handle on the general principles we're discussing, you'll be more comfortable later with the decisions you'll have to make."

"Oh! I just remembered something else," exclaimed Sally.

There was more than one audible groan.

"C'mon, you guys," she said, "this could be important. My insurance pal mentioned something called segregated funds, and you mentioned them briefly. What are they, Uncle Wayne?"

"Segregated funds are similar to mutual funds except they're regulated by the Insurance Act. They offer three unique features. First, they usually guarantee 75% to 100% of your original investment for a certain period of time, usually ten years, or upon death. In addition, you can name a beneficiary for your segregated funds so they don't become part of your estate, which means you'll save money on any estate costs, such as probate. And yes, Sally, we will go over the total estate costs in a later session. A bonus for people like Mark, who owns a business, is that segregated funds may be considered creditor-proof. This means that if Mark gets sued or goes bankrupt, his creditors may not have access to his investments in segregated funds. Segregated funds can also be utilized within an RRSP to provide creditor protection."

"I just thought of a joke," Sally said as she started to laugh. "What is the difference between bonds and men? Eventually, bonds mature! Get it?"

"Ha ha, Sally. So how do our RRSPs and TFSAs fit into the picture?" asked David.

"You're going to have to bribe me for the answer to that one," laughed Uncle Wayne. "I'm starving. Jack, do you think you could do some Cajun hot dogs and get your thirsty old uncle another pop?"

They call my hot dogs Cajun because I tend to burn them. Sally took care of the drinks while I fired up the barbecue and went over the morning's key points in my mind:

1. When allocating your investments requirements, you should answer the following questions:

   - Do you need the cash now to pay off debts or for purchases? (liquidity)
   - Do you need to set up an income plan from the inheritance to fund your current expenses and lifestyle?
   - Is the inheritance earmarked to provide for your future retirement income?

2. The three main types of investments are cash, bonds, and stocks.

   - The risk factors associated with investments include taxes and inflation over the long term, in addition to volatility in the short term.
   - Over the long term, stocks offer the best potential for growth to beat inflation.
   - Asset allocation plays a major role in determining the return on investment.

3. The six key factors in developing a globally diversified portfolio are:

   - strategic asset allocation
   - tactical asset allocation
   - specific investments and/or money managers
   - risk management
   - fees
   - taxes

4. Retirees must create a de-accumulation strategy from the assets they have acquired over their lifetime, from a timing, tax, and sequencing standpoint, as they may have numerous sources of cash-flow, such as:

   - Old Age Security and Canada Pension Plan
   - company pension plans

- RRSPs, RRIFs, locked in RRSPs,
- tax free savings accounts (TFSAs)
- annuities and guaranteed income products,
- non-registered investment accounts.

5. When you make the transition to retirement, you must make sure you have a customized retirement income strategy and cash-flow plan set up, as you have less time to make up for mistakes. The basic strategies to create an income and cash-flow strategy are:

- income only investing
- income focused investing
- life income annuity/guaranteed income products
- total return investing—diversified portfolio
- combination of the above

6. Segregated funds can be a good alternative for people who are nervous about the lack of guarantees when it comes to mutual funds, or for people who require certain creditor protection.

Chapter 4

TAX CONCERNS, RRSPs, AND TFSAs

We were finishing up the Cajun hot dogs when David had the gall to complain that his were a bit more Cajun than usual. I told him that if he didn't keep quiet, he might wind up with a good ol' Louisiana-style blackened steak for dinner that night. That did the trick.

Fortunately, after lunch Jan wanted to take a boat ride down to the harbour and offered to take our kids along. That meant Sandra and I were off the hook for a little while longer and could attend the afternoon session of the "strategy club," as we had begun to call ourselves.

Uncle Wayne started off by saying this wouldn't take any more than forty-five minutes, because he really had to get back to Aunt Jen. Then he told us to pull out our binders or go online to our secure cloud service and look at a tax-related form called a Notice of Assessment. Everyone who files a tax return gets one of these from the Canada Revenue Agency (CRA) every year, but surprise, surprise … Sally couldn't find hers!

Anyway, the point of checking out this form was to determine our limits for RRSP contributions for the current year, and to determine whether we were able to take advantage of any unused contribution limits from the past.

"Well, Sally, if you can't find the form, there's always Plan B. On Monday, you can call the automated TIPS line at the CRA. Just follow the instructions, enter your Social Insurance number, date of birth, plus the figure for your income, which is listed on line 150 of your tax return. They'll tell you what your RRSP limit is. You can also register with the CRA for their My Account service, which allows you to access your information online."

"It's not as if I really cared," she said softly.

"Well, you should," Uncle Wayne said, chiding her gently. "This is where you're going to start. I want everyone to put the maximum allowed this year into their RRSP. And since you've got the cash on hand, do it sooner rather than later. For example, if Sally were to contribute $10,000 a year to her RRSP at the beginning of each year, as opposed to the end of each year, by age sixty-five at a 6.6% annual return, she would have saved $937,312 versus $879,280!"

"I guess RRSPs are a good place to start an investment program, because our money gets tax-sheltered growth," remarked Alice. "But what if we have a large RRSP room? Should we use the tax deduction in our tax return in one year?"

"It depends on your marginal tax rate. Your accountant should be able to review how much you should deduct each year on your tax return to maximize your tax savings," added Uncle Wayne.

"I understand I have to pay taxes, but what is a marginal tax rate?" I asked.

Sandra interjected. "From my understanding, Canada operates under a marginal tax rate system, which means that the more money you make, the more income tax you pay on each additional dollar of income. Simply, as your income rises, the tax rate percentage increases as well, and that is called your marginal tax rate."

"Ok, smarty pants, what about TFSAs? How do they fit in?" I added.

Sandra glared at me and continued. "TFSA stand for Tax Free Savings Account. You don't get any tax deduction for the money you invested into a TFSA; however, you don't pay any tax on the growth of the money in the TFSA, whether it is interest, dividend, and/or capital gains income. And you can take it out tax free. With a TFSA, you can invest in basically the same type of investments as your RRSP. And to make it clear, honey, you never pay tax on the money you earn or take out of a TFSA. How's that, Jack? Are you able to follow that?"

Mark started to laugh, and Uncle Wayne said to save me, "What I would add is that the amount of money you can invest into a TFSA increases each year; however, you have to be eighteen to invest in a TFSA. Here, all of you look at my iPad. TFSAs were introduced in 2009, and you can see how much you can invest per year since then:

- 2009—$5,000
- 2010—$5,000
- 2011—$5,000
- 2012—$5,000
- 2013—$5,500
- 2014—$5,500
- 2015—$10,000
- 2016—$5,500
- 2017—$5,500
- 2018—$5,500
- 2019—$6,000
- 2020—$6,000

"Since all of you were eighteen as of 2009, each of you could have invested up to $69,500 into a TFSA this year. If you take money out of a TFSA, you can re-contribute that amount the following year."

Mark interrupted. "I just want to clarify. Since my oldest turned eighteen in 2014, does that mean he can invest up to $44,000 into an TFSA this year?"

"Wow, and I thought you couldn't do math!" Sally laughed out loud.

"Well, when I was a kid, we didn't have a cell phone with a calculator on it, like you Millennials."

Uncle Wayne continued. "Ok, you two! You're correct on both counts, Mark. I always thought TFSAs were misnamed; they should have been called tax free investment accounts, because with the word 'savings' in there, many people assume you can only invest in saving types of accounts that pay a low interest rate, which is wrong, as you can have growth investments in there as well."

"So how should we allocate our money amongst RRSPs, TFSAs, and non-registered investments?" David asked.

"Whoa! What are non-registered accounts?" Sandra questioned.

"Both are great questions," Uncle Wayne continued. "First of all, RRSPs and TFSAs are considered registered accounts, as they are registered with the government, they have rules and regulations on how much you can invest, and they carry tax consequences, as we have talked about. So an investment that is not placed in an RRSP or TFSA is considered a non-registered investment. It's simply an investment in your name as owner, and each year you pay tax on the income that it earns."

Sandra commented, "I see why it's called a non-registered account."

"To get back to David's question, I would first top up your RRSPs, then maximize your TFSAs, and lastly invest in a non-registered account. That way you can get the tax deduction from your RRSP contribution, and, going forward, both your RRSPs and TFSAs can grow tax free."

"So how do we invest within each type of investment? Do we choose investments that are geared toward growth or toward income?" David asked.

"That's a very good question, and there's no clear-cut answer. Some experts suggest putting all your income type of investments inside your RRSP and TFSA, and investments that bear dividends and capital gains, such as stocks, outside your RRSP/TFSA in a non-registered investment account. Their reasoning is that interest income is taxed at a higher rate than dividends and capital gains, and by being inside your RRSP and TFSA, the interest income is tax-sheltered while it grows. However, with today's low interest rates, it can make sense to have some equity/growth type of investments within your RRSP and TFSA. A common approach is to have the same allocation within your RRSP and TFSA and non-registered account. Again, you must do the math, and this is where your CFP® can help and model the various options.

"You've all told me that you hope to retire somewhere around the age of sixty, but ideally you won't want to activate your RRSP or turn it into a Registered Retirement Income Fund (RRIF) until you're seventy-one, which is the age that an RRSP must be either collapsed or converted to a RRIF or an annuity. It makes sense to have some potential for growth inside your RRSP so that it has maximum value when you're seventy-one, especially when you consider that you could live until you're well past ninety and will need money for a long time."

"What about spousal RRSPs?" David asked. "I was wondering if I should get one for Alice, since she doesn't work yet."

Alice's lower jaw dropped about a foot. "What do you mean I don't work yet?" she sputtered. "Just who do you think raised your children and looked after the house? Honestly, David, sometimes ..."

Uncle Wayne tried to smooth her ruffled feathers. "Of course you work, Alice, and with beautiful results, if the way Scott and Jan behave is any indication. And yes, spousal RRSPs are very important, David, whether the spouse works inside or outside the home. You see, both you and Alice will want to have approximately the same dollar value in your individual RRSPs when you decide to use them. This is called income splitting, and the goal is to pay the least possible amount of tax as you withdraw funds from your RRIFs."

"Let me see if I've got this straight," Alice said. "If David contributes to a spousal RRSP, he gets the tax deduction, and I become the owner. If we don't start a spousal RRSP, he'll have a large RRSP when we retire, but I won't have one at all, because I didn't work outside the home. The total amount in our retirement fund will be the same either way, but as sole owner, David will wind up in a high tax bracket when it's time to withdraw the funds. By using a spousal RRSP, the total taxable income is split between two people at retirement and—voila!— we save on taxes."

"You're getting very good at this," Uncle Wayne said. "Once you're both age sixty-five, you're able to income split income from your RRIFs, and at any age prior, you can split pension income like Sandra has. However, to give you more flexibility, it's still a good idea to try to split assets using spousal RRSPs, as you may need income prior to age sixty-five."

"What about Jack and me?" Sandra asked. "Should Jack contribute to a spousal RRSP for me, even though I have my pension plan as a teacher and we can income split?"

"That depends on the math," Uncle Wayne answered. "You'll want to split income at retirement, so you should project Jack's RRSP to retirement age and figure out how much income it will provide. If that figure is greater than your projected pension income, he should contribute to a spousal RRSP for you. However, if the projections show that your pension income will be greater, you should contribute to an RRSP for Jack and then a spousal RRSP for him."

"Now that's what I call true equality between the sexes!" I said.

"You would!" Sandra countered. "The rest of the world just calls it good financial planning."

"Before we leave the subject of RRSPs and TFSA, I want everyone to look in their binders and tell me how much money you were paying monthly on your debts before you took my excellent advice and paid off all loans that weren't tax deductible. Jack, what were you and Sandra paying every month for your mortgage?"

Sandra had our binder and told everyone our payments had been $1,546 a month. When Uncle Wayne asked if we'd been comfortable with that level of payment, she nodded.

"I'm glad to hear it," Uncle Wayne said, "because you're going to continue making those payments, except now that you're mortgage-free, you'll be making monthly contributions to an RRSP, and please make sure that you set it up in a way that allows you to split income in the future.

"If and when the monthly RRSP contributions meet your allowable limit for the year, you should invest the excess in your TFSAs, followed by your non-registered account in the name of the lower income earner, but keep in mind there are certain attribution rules that you'll have to watch for. You may want to ask your lawyer or accountant about this."

"Why the lower one, and what are attribution rules?" asked Sandra.

"Attribution rules can be tricky, but basically they prevent taxpayers from reducing their taxable income by shifting investment income to a lower taxed person, such as their spouse, kids, or grandkids. If this happens, the income is 'attributed' back to the person who gave them the money, which means they have to pay the tax on that income. Your accountant and CFP® should be able to help you with this. So in the case of a non-registered account, the income it earns each year is taxable, so you want them taxed in the hands of the person in the lower tax bracket," he answered.

"Of course," she reasoned. "By the way, what are the RRSP limits these days?"

"For 2020," replied Uncle Wayne, "the maximum contribution is 18% of your earned income, or $27,230, whichever is less. But remember, Sandra, you have a pension plan at work, so your maximum RRSP contribution every year will be reduced by something called the pension adjustment (P.A.). You'll find that figure on the Notice of Assessment you were looking at earlier."

"Uncle Wayne, I don't know if I have the discipline to put the kind of money you're talking about into an RRSP," Sally admitted. "Although, if Jack and Sandra are accustomed to making the payments anyway, I guess your plan could build a solid portfolio for them. How much would their $1,546 a month be worth at the end of twenty years?"

"Hang on. I'll use my phone calculator," he replied. "Okay. If we assume a payment of $1,546 a month for twenty years into a balanced portfolio with a return of 6.6%, the last twenty-year average return … the answer is … hmm. Who wants to guess?"

"I say about $450,000," ventured Sandra.

"Nope, you're low. The grand total is $753,918. That's the power and magic of compounding," Uncle Wayne told us with a smile.

"So to build a portfolio worth close to $800,000, all Jack and Sandra have to do is continue to make the same dollar payments as they did with their mortgage, but instead put the money into their RRSP and/or TFSA," Sally said in amazement. "That's incredible."

"It sure sounds like the way to go," Sandra added. "But you know something, Uncle Wayne, I still feel a knot in my stomach about investing in the stock market, even if the money's in a diversified portfolio. You say that stocks outperform bonds and GICs in the long term, but I still don't understand why."

"Neither do I," Sally said.

"Well, we've looked at the long-term trends, and I've shown you in black and white that over time the stock market, like the economy, has always gone up," Uncle Wayne explained. "If you really can't cope with the temporary ups and downs of the stock market, then perhaps it isn't for you. I've always felt that people must decide where they fit in the scheme of things when it comes to participating in the economy.

"For example, if you're looking to invest $1,000, you've got several options. You could lend the money to a bank in the form of a GIC, and the bank agrees to pay you interest of 3%. The bank will then lend the money to a company, and the company will pay the bank a higher rate, say 5%. The company has to make a profit greater than 5% on the money it borrowed in order to pay back the bank so that the bank can pay you the interest it promised. So for you to get the guaranteed return from the bank, the bank must invest the money someplace else. So why let the banks make all the money?

"Over the long term, the success of any free market economy depends on companies being productive. If all companies over the long term are not productive and don't make money, the guarantees of GICs and bonds don't mean a thing."

"That makes sense, Uncle Wayne," Sandra commented. "The economy is based on individual companies making money and people buying stuff. So over the long term, some companies will always be successful!"

I told Uncle Wayne I had one further question. "You've helped us review the proper percentages for income and equity investments in each of our portfolios. But since the different types of investments will grow at different rates, won't the percentages go out of whack?"

"I'm glad you asked that, Jack," Uncle Wayne answered, "because that's the last subject I want to tackle in this session: how to rebalance your portfolio.

"I'm sure you've all heard the old saying that the way to make money is to 'buy low and sell high.' The problem is, most Canadians do the exact opposite; they buy high and sell low! The crash of 2008–2009 is a good example. A lot of Canadians had jumped on the bandwagon and invested up to 2007. When the market crashed 2008, some panicked and sold their funds at a loss. In other words, they bought high and sold low.

"Here's another way of looking at it. If the real estate market has been soft for a period of time, and the value of your house has gone down, would that be a good reason to sell your house?"

"That would be crazy," David answered. "Why would we do that? Real estate has always appreciated over the long term."

"Exactly," Uncle Wayne agreed. "But people will bail out of their investments when they see a decline in value, and then they'll buy when prices start going back up. They're doing exactly the opposite of what they should. It's obvious that these people don't have a long-term plan, or a wise old uncle!"

"How do we buy low and sell high?" I asked. "Isn't that what the experts call market-timing?"

"I've got an answer for you that will be easier in the long run. We've already reviewed the various asset allocations based on risk level and goals. Of course, the balance between the equity and income assets you've chosen will shift over time, because the assets grow at a different rate.

"Keep in mind the allocation of the portfolio assets between cash, bonds, and stocks can determine up to 85% of the difference in returns on your investments, so you'll want to make adjustments in your portfolio now and then to keep your ideal balance intact. That's what we call rebalancing your portfolio, and you should do it once a year, or whenever your portfolio shifts out of balance by more than 5% to 10%. This will help you to buy low and sell high."

"I understand the rebalancing concept," Mark said, "but I don't see how it helps us buy low and sell high."

"Ok, I'll give you an example. Let's say you've got $100,000 to invest at the beginning of the year, and your ideal asset allocation is 50/50 between equity/growth and income investments. When the end of the year rolls around, the equity portion might have grown by 10%, so it's worth $55,000. The fixed income may have grown by a different rate, let's say 3%, so their value would be $51,500. Your total portfolio would now be worth $106,500, but the asset allocation would no longer be 50/50, so you're out of balance. To rebalance your portfolio, you'd have to sell off the appropriate amount of growth investments and use the money to purchase income investments. In this case, you want $53,250 invested in each category, so you'd subtract that amount from the value of the equity funds to tell you how much capital you need to move to guaranteed investments in order to rebalance your portfolio. By the way, the answer is $1,750. By doing this, you would have sold some growth investments at a high dollar value; in other words, you have 'bought low, and sold high,' and you've protected some of your profits."

"So," I reasoned, "if stocks were going through a temporary lull, and the income portion had increased in value more than the equity portion, then we'd have to rebalance by buying equity investments with a portion of the proceeds with the fixed income investments."

"Of course," Sandra added. "That makes perfect sense. If you're going to buy stocks, buy low, when they haven't gone through a spurt in growth."

Uncle Wayne looked at us with pride. "I'm glad you get it. By rebalancing your portfolio yearly, or whenever it's out of balance, by 5% to 10%, you automatically buy low and sell high. People who did this in 2008 really benefited during the upturn starting in 2009."

"Uncle Wayne," Alice interjected, "I'm surprised that you haven't recommended that we spread the purchase of our initial investment over a period of twelve to eighteen months. The books I've been reading say we should ease into the market slowly. Prices could vary quite a bit over that year and a half, and by investing all at once, we might be buying high!"

"Well done, Alice," he replied. "With all the extra research you've been doing, you may want to lead the session next week."

"Before you go," Sandra said, "I have one last question. Whose name should our investments be in, mine or Jack's?"

"From a strictly legal point of view, an inheritance is not considered part of family or matrimonial property, which we will look at later. But the lines get fuzzy once you start paying off mortgages or purchasing spousal RRSPs. It gets hard to tell just whose money was used for what, and once you start mingling the funds, they may be considered matrimonial property in the event of divorce. Not that you two will ever come to that!

"We're going to delve a bit deeper into the topic of who owns what in one of our future sessions when we talk about estate planning. In the meantime, just go by what we talked about earlier. For the lump sum inheritance, from a legal standpoint, it should only be invested in the name of the person who inherited, but for the monthly investments going forward, use RRSPs for your monthly investments until you reach your contribution limits, and then invest in each of your TFSAs, followed by a non-registered account in the name of the lower income-earner so that you'll be splitting income.

"And now, I'm going home to see my wife."

"What's the plan for the golf tournament next weekend?" Mark asked.

"Well, the tournament starts at 10:00 a.m., so why don't you come by to get me at about 8:00 a.m. That'll give us all time to get warmed up, so you won't have any excuses when I beat you!"

In the car as we made our way home from the cottage that weekend, we got stuck in traffic around Barrie again. Paige and Connor had both fallen asleep, so Sandra and I reviewed the key issues from Saturday afternoon's session:

1. We should review taking advantage of our RRSP limit.
2. TFSAs are the next location for investments.
3. Use spousal RRSPs in order to split income at retirement.
4. Invest the money we used to pay into our mortgage into a monthly RRSP investment plan.
5. When we have reached our RRSP limits, put the monthly investment into each of our TFSAs, followed then into a non-registered account in the name of the lower income earner.
6. Model and review what are the best long-term solutions to allocate our investments type within our RRSPs, TFSAs, and non-registered accounts.
7. Buy low and sell high by rebalancing our portfolio on a yearly basis, or whenever it shifts more than 5% to 10% away from the recommended balance between income and stock/equity investments.
8. Consider spreading the initial investment in the growth portion of our portfolio over a period of twelve to eighteen months.

Chapter 5

PROTECTING YOUR FAMILY

The following weekend, Sandra and I woke up early on Saturday. The water was still, and the sun was just beginning to burn off the morning haze.

We decided to slip down to the water for a quick swim before the kids woke up. When we reached the dock, we saw Mark and Aunt Lorraine preparing for their Saturday morning ritual dip.

Mark yelled over, "I hope you're hungry, because I'm cooking this morning."

"I hope you can cook better than you golf!" Sandra shouted back.

Mark pretended not to hear.

We all made the trek over to Aunt Lorraine's and found Mark at the barbecue grilling sausages and back bacon. Aunt Lorraine was busy inside making waffles, and soon we were all munching happily and sitting on the deck overlooking the bay.

Alice couldn't resist giving Mark a backhanded compliment. "This is pretty good," she said. "Maybe if you started offering breakfast as part of a package deal, you'd be able to get a date."

Aunt Lorraine smiled fondly at them both and announced that she wanted to go down to the harbour to pick up the Saturday newspaper. Even though she could read it on her iPad, she still liked the feel of the newsprint. Scott and Jan volunteered to go with her and take Connor and Paige along for the ride.

After they left, we started to talk while we waited for Uncle Wayne.

"I hate life insurance," David grumbled. "It's just too complicated. I have a policy through work, and coupled with my inheritance, that ought to be enough. I hope this session doesn't take too long."

As soon as we heard Uncle Wayne start his boat, Sally and Alice went down to the dock to greet him while Mark brought out the coffee and some cinnamon buns in case he was hungry.

"I can smell those rolls already," Uncle Wayne bellowed as he made his way up toward the cottage. "I sure hope there will be enough for the rest of you after I've had my fill."

As soon as he sat down, Uncle Wayne took a sip of coffee, grabbed a roll with great flourish, and announced that the session was on.

"Now, let's see what you know about life insurance. Open your binders and tell me whether you think you are underinsured or over insured."

"If you ask anyone who sells life insurance, they'll tell you there's no such thing as being over insured," Sandra commented.

"I've heard the same thing, Sandra, and sometimes I wonder if it isn't all just one big con game," David remarked. "Besides, now that we've inherited some money, why do we need life insurance at all?"

"Maybe you don't," Uncle Wayne answered, although his tone wasn't the least bit convincing. "Tell you what, let's double check for the sake of your family. There's no reason to be over insured, but if you pull all the papers out of your binders relating to your group policies and any individual life insurance policies, we can determine whether you need additional life insurance after we factor your inheritance into the equation."

David still seemed reluctant. "Okay, fine. How do we figure out how much insurance we should have?"

Sally was first in with an answer. "The amount of life insurance you need is directly linked to the amount of capital it would take to:

1. pay off all your debts;
2. provide for your children's education;
3. pay your final taxes, including capital gains taxes;
4. provide enough income to comfortably support your dependents when the remainder is invested; and
5. create a legacy for your family and/or for a favourite cause or charity.

"What you have to remember is that you're not really insuring a life, but rather the income that the life would have produced."

Mark did a double take. "Where did you learn all that?"

"Think back," she answered. "You might remember that one of my old boyfriends was an insurance salesman."

"I remember him," I laughed. "His name was Mike, and he came up to the cottage about two years ago. He was a wild one, the only guy I ever remember going skinny-dipping on the May 24 weekend."

"Hello," Sandra said, waving her hand about. "Can we please get back on track? What was that bit about capital gains taxes?"

Uncle Wayne answered. "When someone dies, Revenue Canada assumes that he or she has sold all their assets at fair market value the day before the actual date of death. So if an applicable non-registered asset has gone up in value from its purchase price, it is deemed to have produced a capital gain. Fifty per cent of all capital gains are taxable upon the individual's death, and those capital gains taxes are included as part of the person's final tax bill. However, please remember that this does not apply to a spouse, as assets can be rolled over to a spouse tax free. Sometimes this is called a spousal rollover."

"For Dad's estate, we had to pay capital gains taxes on his non-registered mutual fund holdings," I explained, "and on the cottage, since it was not Dad's principal residence, even though it hadn't actually been sold.

"The amount of money that was in his RRIFs was included as income in the year of death. There was no tax on his home, which was his principal residence. That's just the way the system works."

"Now let's find out whether or not you have enough life insurance," Uncle Wayne said. "Jack, you start."

"I think I'm looking pretty good," I said brightly. "I've got my own permanent life policy for $100,000, and then there's my policy at the office through the group benefits plan, and that's worth about $100,000."

"Well, since Jack has both a term policy and a permanent life policy, let's use him as an example to determine if he has the required amount of insurance for what he wants to do."

"Wait a minute, Uncle Wayne. What's the difference between term and a permanent life insurance policy?" Sandra asked.

Uncle Wayne explained. "The difference is sort of like the difference between renting and buying a home. An apartment will satisfy your short-term needs, and you'll pay less every month, but you're not building any equity. When you buy a house, the mortgage may cost you more on a monthly basis, but at the end of twenty-five years, the payments are finished, and you own it."

"Okay, that sort of makes sense. Term life insurance is like renting, and permanent life insurance is like buying a home. So for shorter-term needs, you use term life insurance, and for longer-term or permanent needs, you use permanent life insurance. Is that correct?" Sandra added.

Uncle Wayne smiled and continued. "That's a good summary. Okay, Jack, let's proceed. First, if anything happened to you, what would you want to leave behind for Sandra, Connor, and Paige?"

"To tell you the truth, I haven't thought about it all that much. However, based on what Sally said earlier, I suppose I'd need to leave enough capital to ensure that, when invested, it would produce a yearly income equal to the income I produced when I was alive. How much capital would that be, anyway?"

"I'm looking at the Government of Canada life insurance calculator," Alice said while looking at her iPad. "Let's fill it in using your circumstances. What additional living expenses on top of what Sandra earns would she need?"

"It's probably safe to say that Sandra needs another $35,000 a year after tax on top of her own salary to support the kind of lifestyle she and the kids are used to."

"Speaking of the kids, have you started their education funds yet?" Sally asked.

"No, we haven't. Mark, your kids are in university now. What do you figure it's costing you?"

"Well, I'd say the full cost these days for four years is somewhere in the $100,000 range, assuming they want to go away to school," he answered.

Uncle Wayne said, "I assume that after our discussion a few weeks ago you're no longer carrying any debt, right?"

Sandra and I both nodded. "And we have no capital gains considerations," I added, "because our only investments are the house and our RRSPs."

"Okay," Sally continued, "so I have entered that you have $200,000 of life insurance. You need $35,000 a year for twenty years of additional income/spending, and you need about $200,000 for an education fund, and the answer is that you need another $700,000 of life insurance."

"That's incredible!" Sandra sputtered. "Surely Jack doesn't need that much insurance."

"Should I also deduct the value of our RRSPs and the house?" I asked.

Alice jumped in. "No, don't include your RRSPs, because you would have to pay about 50% in taxes if you had to liquidate them now. If you leave Sandra as the beneficiary of your RRSPs, they'll then become RRSPs in her name. There will be no taxes payable until she starts withdrawing funds after she retires."

Then it was Uncle Wayne's turn again. "That's correct, Alice, and we'll discuss this later when we cover minimizing estate costs. To get back on track, what about the second part of your question, Jack? Would you want Sandra to sell the house?"

"I most certainly hope not!" Sandra interjected before I could even open my mouth.

"Of course not," I agreed. "I'd want them to keep the house, and all their wonderful memories of me along with it! So if I'm not including the value of the house or the RRSPs, that means that all I really deduct from the $700,000 is what's left of the inheritance, which is about $50,000 after paying off our mortgage, so I need another $650,000. Well, Uncle Wayne, I guess you would say I'm underinsured. Seriously underinsured."

"If we had a policy that size on Jack, what would happen if he was hit by lightning on the golf course?" Sandra asked. "Do I just notify the insurance company? Do they send a cheque for the full amount? Do they hold back any taxes?"

"You sound a little anxious, dear," I remarked. "However, I happen to know that life insurance proceeds come tax-free. All you would have to do is invest the money wisely to provide an income for yourself and the kids ... well, that and visit my grave frequently. By the way, how come I'm the one who has to die?"

"When your number's up, you go!" David said with a laugh. "And since Jack's on his way out, what kind of additional insurance should he buy? Right now, he's got both permanent and term insurance."

"The answer depends mainly on timing," Uncle Wayne replied. "Sandra, how long would you need Jack's income if you were raising the kids alone?"

"Hmmm, I guess about twenty years, maybe less, but certainly until they're in university and I could return to work full time."

"Well, if you would only need the money for twenty years, then Jack only needs the life insurance protection for a twenty-year period. In this kind of situation, I'd recommend term insurance," Uncle Wayne told us.

"Why term and not permanent life insurance?" I asked. "Doesn't term insurance get more expensive as you get older?"

"Yes, it does. But remember, you're young now, and you only need this coverage for twenty years. After that, you needn't worry about life insurance to replace your income, because your kids will be fully grown, and Sandra would be able to support herself by working full time. You might also wish to add a contingency fund, as it may take Sandra a few years to get her income level up to what is needed. At your age, term insurance is going to be cheaper if the period it spans is twenty years or less."

"As usual, Uncle Wayne, you're making a lot of sense," I said with admiration. "I'll look into additional term insurance this week to make sure my family's need for income replacement is covered."

"Good stuff," Uncle Wayne replied. "Now, how much life insurance do you have on Sandra?"

"Just her basic policy through work. Is that a problem?"

"Could be. How would you replace her income if anything happened to her? And do you have any idea how much it would cost to provide full time daycare for Connor and Paige, or for that matter, hire a live-in nanny?"

"I haven't got a clue," I replied, looking over at Sandra. "It's not something we've ever considered."

"Well, you really should." It was a gentle reprimand. "I think it's a good idea to insure all working spouses, and I would definitely include someone who stays at home to look after the kids in my definition of a spouse who works. I'm sure Alice would agree. Anyway, by doing this, you will have covered all the bases in case something should happen to either one of you."

David was starting to lose his skepticism. "Let me make sure I've got this straight. We need enough insurance to pay off all liabilities, final taxes, including capital gains taxes, and provide an income for the family, as well as care for the kids, and create a legacy if I wish to?"

Uncle Wayne nodded, so David continued. "From my binder of what I own and owe, I can ascertain:

1. the after-tax income my family needs to maintain our current lifestyle,
2. the amount of money that I owe (debts),
3. estimated education costs,
4. potential capital gains and final taxes, and
5. legacy desires.

"This much I understand," he said, "but I'm still not clear on the difference between permanent life insurance and term life insurance. Somebody tell me again why term insurance is the best buy for Jack."

JACK LUMSDEN, MBA, CFP®

"I'll try, but the best buy really depends on your age, how long you'll need the insurance, and the purpose behind getting it," Sally said. "As we discussed, since Jack only needs the insurance for about a twenty-year time period, and cost is a factor, term life insurance is the way to go. Remember the analogy that the difference is sort of like the difference between renting and buying a home, where term is renting, and permanent is owning?"

Sally then went online to an insurance company site and started to enter the information for a non-smoking forty-year old born March 1, 1979, and came up with the following cost for twenty-year term insurance. She told us the estimated annual premium I would pay for a $650,000 20-term policy:

AGE	TWENTY YEAR TERM
40–60	$ 709—annual premium
61–80	$10,146—annual premium

"That premium isn't too bad until age sixty," I commented, "but after sixty it gets expensive. Uncle Wayne, do we have any value in the policy after we've paid into it for twenty years?"

"No, Jack, no value. All you have is the insurance coverage as long as you pay the premium, but once you stop, the coverage stops, and you have no cash value. If you wanted to use the life insurance to create a larger estate, or to pay potential taxes down the road, you would have to invest in a permanent life insurance plan, but the annual premium would be more."

"Why the price difference?" asked David.

Sally answered his question with one of her own. "Would you agree that regardless of which type of life insurance Jack buys, his chances of dying remain the same?"

"Sure."

"Insurance companies think so too. With a permanent life policy, the company invests the amount of money paid over and above what's paid on the pure life insurance costs, and then permanent life policy holders share in the profits from the investments. And you don't have to pay any income tax on the build-up of the cash value over time."

"I see," David said. "So that's where the cash value of a permanent life insurance policy comes from, and it can provide some tax advantages."

Sandra had a quizzical look on her face. "Let me get this straight. With term insurance, your coverage stops as soon as you stop paying the premiums, whether it's after one year or twenty. There's no pay-out, unless of course the reason you stopped paying your premiums is that you happened to die. However, with permanent life insurance, you may have built up some 'cash value' with your policy."

David looked thoughtful. "I'm with you now. Jack only needs to provide an income for his family for the next fifteen to twenty years, so he only needs life insurance for that period."

"By George, you've got it!" exclaimed Uncle Wayne.

"So, Jack," David said with a grin, "it looks like you were sold a bill of goods when you bought that permanent life policy."

"Not really, brother dear," Sally added. "Permanent life insurance does have its place in a financial plan. It can be used to create a larger estate for your family or to support your favourite cause or charity. Again, this is from my insurance agent friend."

"Don't worry about it, Jack." Uncle Wayne stepped in to soothe my feelings. "A lot of families are underinsured, and just as many buy the wrong type of life insurance for their needs. It's a complicated business, but permanent life insurance is a smart buy when the need for insurance is going to last an entire lifetime, which is the case when you're covering off the potential for taxes on capital gains or for a charity. In fact, I have a permanent life insurance policy, which I'm leaving to the greatest university in the world, Wilfrid Laurier University. In one of our later sessions, we'll talk about a situation where permanent life insurance is an essential part of estate planning."

"Hey," David ventured, "I went to Western. It's the best university in Canada."

"Now, David, we all know that Western sucks!" I howled as I got up to gather another cup of coffee. "You know, I went to WLU as well, with my friend Frank. Whenever one of us would say 'Western,' the other would say 'Sucks!'

"What are you, like fourteen years old, Jack?" David said with grin on his face, as this was not the first time he'd heard this.

Mark finally got back into the conversation. "I don't think I need any life insurance, since I don't have any liabilities, and I've already provided for my children's education. I don't imagine that Sally needs life insurance either, at least not at this point in her life."

Alice looked piercingly at Mark. "Are you saying that you don't have any capital gains exposure? Not even with your business?"

"Gee, I hadn't thought of that. I'd better check with my accountant. I can see that permanent insurance could be a great solution for my capital gains exposure. Thanks, Alice."

"There's one other detail I forgot to mention earlier," Uncle Wayne said. "There is a not for profit life insurance company organization called Assuris, and it protects policy holders in the event a life insurance company fails. If this happens, the policy will be transferred to a solvent life insurance company, if it's a member of Assuris. The amount of coverage that will be transferred is up to $200,000 per person, or 85% of the promised value, whichever is higher, per company."

"That's a pretty important point," I commented, "especially since I may be buying term insurance worth $650,000."

"You should also do some research and use only companies with the strongest financial position," added Uncle Wayne.

"How about disability insurance?" Alice asked. "Do you think we need any on David, or are we okay now that we have his inheritance?"

"You're getting too sharp for the rest of us," Uncle Wayne replied. "I almost forgot about that, along with most of the rest of the population."

Sally perked up and once again displayed her considerable knowledge on the subject. "Everyone should have disability insurance. If you can't perform your job due to an accident or illness, it pays you up to 65% or 70% of your regular income. Most people who work for large companies may have some disability coverage through group plans, but the coverage may be limited, and you might want to consider an individual plan custom-tailored to your needs."

"Well now," I said, "what does our insurance expert have to say about Employment Insurance, and the Workers' Compensation Plan?"

"These are very basic plans, Jack. A pay-out from EI only lasts from about fourteen weeks to a maximum of forty-five weeks, depending on where you live, while Workers' Compensation only covers on-the-job accidents, and besides, when you look at the deficits so many governments are racking up, do you really think you can rely on them to take care of you?"

"I wouldn't," I laughed, "unless of course I was a Member of Parliament and could give myself an indexed pension, where I get a lifetime guaranteed income that can increase every year with inflation when I retire."

"Do you think I need disability insurance?" Mark asked.

Sally was starting to run out of patience. "If you couldn't do your job, a disability policy would pay you a monthly income so you could cover your bills, buy food, and put gas in the boat. Perhaps you'd rather use your inheritance to pay for those things, and risk the comfortable retirement you had planned, while leaving behind less money for your kids. It's your choice."

"Okay then," Mark asked, "under what circumstances would I not need disability insurance?"

"You could forgo a disability policy if your financial assets would produce approximately the same income that you earn on the job. Your ability to earn an income over the years is really your largest asset, and it should be insured. By the way, at your age you have a greater chance of becoming disabled than you do of dropping dead."

"Isn't that a lovely thought," I said.

"What about our policies through work?" asked Sandra.

Uncle Wayne handled this one. "If I were you, I would find out what the monthly benefit would be, and how the policy defines the word 'disability.' If the policy doesn't provide about 65% of your current income, you should at least investigate buying an individual plan to top it up. Assuris protection provides guarantees for disability policies, but only up to $2,000 per month per payment. So as we discussed in the case of life insurance, you should not only look at the premiums but the strength of the insurance company."

Sally grabbed another cup of coffee and asked Uncle Wayne, "What do you think about critical illness insurance? My friend mentioned it to me."

"Well, Sally, critical illness insurance pays out a lump sum if you have a heart attack, stroke, or develop cancer, as well as covering some of other medical issues, depending on the company. I've had a few friends who had prostate cancer and it has paid out, which was valuable, as it covered the short time they were off work. It's something that I think you all should review with your financial advisor and see how it could fit into your plans."

Sally continued. "He also mentioned long term care insurance. I'm searching it right know, and the Sun Life Financial web site says, 'Long Term Care Insurance helps you manage the risk of losing your independence due to an unexpected illness, chronic condition or dementia by transferring the risk to Long Term Care Insurance. It provides a comprehensive income-style benefit when you're dependent. It's designed to help cover the cost of care services you need in any environment, including, your personal residence, a retirement home and a long- term care facility.'[3] What does this really mean?"

"Well, Sally, as you get older, and if you're unable to care for yourself and/or have a cognitive condition like Alzheimer's, the insurance company will provide you a weekly or monthly payment to help cover the extra costs for care at home or in a facility. You really must look at the specific company policy to see what you may be covered for. This type of policy must be reviewed carefully as part of your entire retirement and income plan.

"We've talked about why you need insurance, but we haven't really discussed why you may want insurance, as it can be a very useful tool for tax sheltering income and for potentially generating retirement income."

"How does that work, Uncle Wayne?" asked Sally

"Well, simply, the extra money that you pay into a permanent life insurance policy above the cost of insurance can grow tax free. For example, some of my friends with large investment portfolios have transferred some of their conservative, higher taxed investments into a permanent policy. Once inside the policy, the funds grow tax free, and if structured properly, it can pay out tax free to the beneficiaries. With this strategy, my friends pay less tax today and reduced tax on death.

---

[3]   Source: www.sunlife.ca, Sun Long Term Care Insurance

"As for income, if they decide they wish or need to generate income from the permanent policy, they can borrow from it to create tax effective income."

"That sounds complicated," I added.

"Well, it can be, which is why you need an insurance expert who can help you make sure your insurance strategies are in alignment with your financial and estate plan.

"And, my young friends, I think that thoroughly covers the topic of insurance. By the way, your Aunt Jen asked me to invite all of you over to our cottage for breakfast next Saturday. She's been complaining that she never sees you anymore! As for me, I've seen quite enough of you for today, and I'm off to play golf. During the coming week, I want you to make sure you have enough insurance coverage, and then you can review your wills and powers of attorney documents for our next session."

With that, Uncle Wayne headed down the stairs and toward the dock, with Sally and Alice close behind. Sandra went back to our cottage while David and I helped Mark clean up the breakfast dishes.

As we clattered around in the kitchen, we summarized the major points from our discussion about insurance:

1. Many people underestimate the amount of insurance they need and/or buy the wrong kind.

    •   For short-term needs (less than twenty years), buy term insurance.
    •   For needs that last a lifetime, consider permanent life insurance.

2. Families with young children should insure both spouses.
3. You are not really insuring a life but rather the income that the life could produce. In the case of spouses who stay at home to care for children, you are insuring the cost of replacing that care.

4. The insurance policy should provide enough money to:

   - pay all debts;
   - cover the cost of university for the children;
   - pay final taxes, including those on capital gains;
   - replace a person's income and/or provide for daycare or a nanny in the case of spouses who provide childcare in the home; and
   - provide for a legacy if desired.

5. Everyone needs disability insurance, which will replace your income if you can't perform your job.
6. The only circumstance under which you wouldn't need disability insurance is if the investment income from your financial assets equals the income you're able to earn.
7. Verify that your disability coverage at work provides about 65% of your earned income. If it doesn't, consider topping up your coverage with an individual plan.
8. Be sure to review critical illness insurance and long term care insurance to see if they are required in your financial plan.
9. Be aware that Assuris will transfer a policy to another life insurance company if a life insurance company fails, but only within certain limits. Protect your family by using a financially strong life insurance company.
10. Even with an inheritance, the ability to earn an income over the span of an average working life is most people's largest asset.
11. A permanent life insurance policy can be a good financial tool to tax shelter income today and to potentially generate income in retirement.
12. A permanent life insurance policy is also a great tool for business owners to pay for capital gains exposure for their estate and/ or family.
13. An insurance expert can help you tailor your plan to your specific needs and make sure it's aligned with your financial and estate plan.

Chapter 6

ESTATE PLANNING—WILLS AND POWERS OF ATTORNEY

Sandra and I had just finished the dishes on Friday night at the cottage, while Sally was playing with Connor and Paige out on the screened-in porch. We were all waiting for David's family to arrive, and Sandra was a bit nervous because it was already quite dark.

I tried to calm her fears. "Don't worry. David's been driving boats around in the dark up here since he was a kid. We'd go to parties and come home at all hours. Besides, you and I had some memorable moments cruising around in the moonlight ourselves when we were younger. Remember the time that ..."

"I'd stop right now if I were you. I don't remember any moonlight cruises, Jack."

"I think I hear the boat," I said, hoping to diffuse the tension.

"And I think I hear the sound of a desperate man," she answered. "Let's change the subject. After last week's session on insurance, I'm wondering if we've taken the proper steps to make sure we'd be okay if something bad happened. For instance, you could easily fall off the deck this weekend and become horribly disfigured or disabled. And if that happens, accidentally or otherwise, I want to know if you've got enough insurance to fully protect me and the kids."

"This isn't something you're planning, I hope."

"We'll see," she said. "But seriously, have we got all the bases covered?"

"Well, if I were to fall, or get pushed off the deck tonight, the extra term life insurance we applied for this past week would provide enough income to maintain our current standard of living for you and the kids. And we're looking into getting enough life insurance on you to cover the money you make as a part-time teacher and to cover the cost of a nanny to look after the kids if you can't."

"That reminds me," Sandra said, "I checked with our human resources manager at school this week, and I do have disability coverage through work. How about you?"

"I have a basic group policy, but it doesn't provide coverage to 65% of my annual income. What I need is an individual policy to top it up so that a full 65% of what I really make in an average year is covered."

"A sudden accident must make life really tough for people with no disability insurance," Sandra remarked. "I would imagine the cost of caring for someone who is disabled, added to the loss of that person's income, could destroy a family, and even some people might think they'd be better off dead."

"Not me," I said. "If I became disabled, I'd expect you to feed me, dress me, and take me to the Hamilton Tiger-Cats games."

"And how would my life change?" she laughed. "I do those things now. Anyhow, let's get back to the issues at hand. If we were both killed, we have enough insurance in place to make sure Connor and Paige are taken care of for the next twenty years, right?"

"Yup. They'd be well off, and their affairs would be well managed."

"Since you insist on bringing up the subject of affairs, let's revisit the topic of your moonlight cruises," Sandra said. "Specifically, I'd like to know more about your companion. Or is that companions?"

"I'm sure I hear the boat," I said as I flipped on the outside lights and headed toward the door. "I'd better help David land. You know how much trouble he has in the dark."

THE NEXT DAY

The rain was beating down when we woke up on Saturday morning, so Sandra and I decided there was no morning swim for us. As usual, we could hear Mark yell as he jumped into the water off his dock. He always does that when we don't join him for an early morning dip. He's either trying to make us feel like wimps for not going in, or trying to make sure that we're awake, but Connor and Paige usually take care of that much earlier.

After I got dressed, we all made our way down to the dock. We had to take two boats, since there were nine of us going over to Uncle Wayne's for breakfast.

David, Scott, and I climbed into the small tin outboard. Even with equality between the sexes, there are some things that the men are still expected to do, and toughing it out in the open boat when it's cold and rainy is one of them.

Aunt Jen's muffins would be our reward, and we could detect their wonderful aroma, mingled with the scent of coffee brewing, as we made our way up the stairs. It would be a tight squeeze in their cottage today, since we usually ate outside on the deck.

Aunt Jen was awfully cheery for such a dismal day. "Tell me, is your old uncle making any sense so far, or are you just here for my blueberry muffins?"

"Both," David replied.

"I'll second that," added Sally. "Good food plus good ideas. You know, Aunt Jen, there are plenty of financial planning books on the market, but none of them tell you what to do if you get a relatively large sum of money all at once."

Sandra nodded in agreement. "Uncle Wayne's been great, and we really have been taking action based on his advice."

"You'd better stop now," laughed Aunt Jen. "If your uncle's head gets any more swollen, we won't be able to get him out through the door later!"

Throughout the remainder of our breakfast, we relived highlights of the infamous golf tournament and discussed our various schedules for the rest of the summer. After breakfast, Aunt Jen and Aunt Lorraine offered to take the kids up to the cabin to play for an hour or so while the rest of us concentrated on our strategy session. I started reminiscing aloud about the games I had played with David, Mark, and Sally on rainy days at the cottage when we were kids. Our favourites had been Monopoly and Memory.

"Speaking of memory," Sandra interrupted, "who wants to tell me about the girl Jack used to take on moonlight cruises?"

I glanced warily at David and Sally. "Remember our code of silence, you two! And remember what happens if you break it."

"Gee, Sandra, I don't remember any girls before you," David said, smiling sweetly.

"He's right," Sally added. "You were the first woman Jack brought to the cottage. Now let's get started. I've got to get down to the harbour by noon to pick up a friend."

"Is this the guy who likes to skinny dip at midnight?" asked Mark.

"No, it's not. And I'd appreciate you not mentioning that particular incident, thank you."

"I see. So is this a new boyfriend or one of the old standbys?" Mark countered. "I have so much trouble keeping up with your social life."

"At least I have a social life," she shot back.

Uncle Wayne called for a truce. "That's enough, you two. Let's look at your wills. Is everyone's up to date?

David and Alice looked embarrassed and admitted that neither had ever made a will at all.

Sally's eyes narrowed in bewilderment. "David, I can't believe you don't have a will. Despite all the cracks you make, you must think that the government will do a better job of dividing up your assets than you could. And apparently you want your estate taxes to be as high as possible, and you don't care if your family has difficulty gaining access to your assets. I'm sure the government would do a better job managing your estate than ..."

"Okay, Sally, I get your point. It's just something we've put off, mainly because we find it awkward to talk about dying."

"Most people do," Uncle Wayne said, "but you've got to talk about it, and you've got to have wills drawn up. Each province is different, but in Ontario, here's what will happen if someone dies without a will and they have children. If someone has one child, the first $200,000 goes to the spouse, and the balance is split equally between the spouse and child. If you have more than one child, such as you do, Alice would be entitled to the first $200,000 of your estate plus the next one-third of your estate. The rest would be divided between your two children. If the children are under the age of eighteen, the Children's Law Office would get involved.

"That's it, David," Alice said in a resigned tone of voice. "We're seeing our lawyer about wills this week. I suppose we should also name a trustee for Scott and Jan, in case we die at the same time."

"Maybe Jack and Sandra's experience would be helpful to you. What kind of instructions did you two outline in your wills?" Uncle Wayne asked.

"Well, first of all, we named one another as executors of our individual estates, and we also named Sandra's parents as guardians. We decided to use a professional trustee and named a trust company as trustee. The trust could continue for a number of years; we didn't want her parents to be burdened with that as they aged, or potentially be put in conflict with their grandkids over money if they had to manage that for them.

"In addition, we left detailed instructions as to how we want the estate managed. We've left specific instructions with the trustees to use the income to care for Connor and Paige. We've asked that they not withdraw capital while the kids are growing up, unless in their discretion they believe it is in their best interest or they are required to. We also specified that both children receive 50% of their inheritance when they reach the age of twenty-five, and the rest at age thirty."

"Why did you do that?" asked Alice.

"If there's no age specified, they would receive their entire inheritance at the age of eighteen, and both Sandra and I feel that's just too young to handle the responsibility that comes with a huge chunk of money. Remember, we have more than a million dollars' worth of insurance between us, and we worry that the kids might blow it if they get their hands on it too early in life. This way, they get a more than decent sum at age twenty-five, and even if they do blow it, they get a second chance when they're thirty."

"We did something else," Sandra chimed in. "We've asked my mom and dad not to let the kids know while they're growing up that they'll eventually inherit a lot of money. We want them to be secure in the knowledge that their education will be paid for, but that's all. We hope Connor and Paige will become self-sufficient, responsible adults, and we think they'll have a better chance at doing it if they didn't know about a future inheritance while they're young."

"Two great things Dad did was that he had a digital estate plan, which was basically a listing of all the passwords of his online accounts so that I could cancel them. He also introduced me to his certified financial planner, which made it easier as both power of attorney and executor," I added.

"Very good," commented Uncle Wayne. "Now, Mark, who's the executor of your will?"

Mark started leafing through his binder to find the answer, and David used the lull to ask about the role and duties of an executor.

"The executor is responsible for the administration of the estate on behalf of the deceased in accordance with the terms of the will," Sally said quickly.

"Show off!" Mark said. "This new friend of yours must be a lawyer. Okay, I've found my will." As he glanced through the document, his face turned red and his eyes got wider and wider. We all looked at him intently.

"You won't believe this. My executor is still my ex-wife. And yes, Alice, before you ask, my will also leaves everything to her."

Alice chuckled. "I guess everyone should review their wills periodically as their circumstances change."

"Well, this sure isn't what I want. I realize that under the Succession Law Reform Act that she's entitled to 50% of all the assets we accumulated during the marriage, but that was all settled long ago. How do I go about changing my will?" asked Mark.

"I'm glad you brought up the Succession Law Reform Act," Uncle Wayne answered, "because you should all know that it overrides any terms laid down in a will. It also revokes the appointment of power of attorney and appointment as executor if divorced. However, you can make a new will at any time, and one of the first clauses you include is that you are rescinding the terms of your old will. It also provides that if you divorce, your spouse is deemed to have predeceased you for the purposes of your will. So you see, Mark, the government may be smarter than you think. They also believe that an individual would not want to leave any portion of his or her inheritance to a spouse after a divorce, unless it specifically provides otherwise, and figure that there are people like you who forget about changing their wills, so they in a sense do it for you. Also, marriage revokes an existing will, but you will want to review this all with your own lawyer, as it can get complicated!"

"Wow, maybe I've been too tough on the government. But who would you suggest I name as executor? I don't have a wife anymore, and my kids are just in their early twenties and not particularly knowledgeable about finances. I guess Mom knows a lot about money, but she's getting older, and she probably wouldn't want the job."

Uncle Wayne replied that there are several ways to go, but that the most common choices for executor include:

- spouse
- children, if capable
- friend or business associates
- trust company

"What are the pros and cons of each?" Sally wondered.

"If you're married and your estate is fairly straightforward, then naming your spouse is usually the easiest and cheapest route, provided he or she is up to the job."

"If one of your children are old enough, and capable, then that could also be a good choice, but you have to be aware that it could create problems. Sometimes children who act as executors become very controlling regarding money that's been left by one parent to the other, especially when it eventually will go to the kids. Also, family rivalries can crop up when one child has control over an asset that is owned by the entire family, such as a cottage.

"As an alternative, you can name a friend or business associate as your executor, as long as there's no conflict of interest over any of the estate assets.

"Trust companies are always an option too. They're certainly very knowledgeable when it comes to their duties and responsibility as an executor. They'll have all the contacts and processes in place to handle the estate, and they're completely independent, which some people will want. An added feature is that since they're an institution, you don't have to worry about your executor passing away before you do. However, they will almost certainly charge the maximum fees allowed by law for their work in settling the estate."

"Are executor's fees high enough to really matter?" Mark asked.

"It depends on the size of the estate," replied Uncle Wayne. "They can be up to 5% of the assets passing through the will, and then there may also be ongoing costs if the inheritance is not distributed to the beneficiaries right away. In a later session, we'll review more about this, but assets that have a named beneficiary, such as life insurance, RRSPs/RRIFs, and TFSAs, do not pass through the will, and the same goes for joint assets."

"Okay," Alice said. "Going back to Mark's situation ... how about a compromise? Would it make sense for him to name his kids as co-executors along with one of his own friends or business colleagues who know more about financial matters?"

"I like it," Mark said. "As much as I hate to admit it, you're getting pretty good at this stuff."

"Yes, I think it's a good solution for Mark's situation," Uncle Wayne added. "Now, tell me what you've done about signing a power of attorney."

"I know I signed them, but I'm not really sure what it means," Mark admitted.

I tried to give him some answers. "A power of attorney allows someone to look after another person's affairs if that person becomes either unable or incapable of doing it himself. Remember when Dad was in the hospital? He was certainly capable of making decisions, his mind was fine, but he wasn't able to physically go to the bank and make deposits, withdrawals, or transfers, as he wasn't online for all his accounts. He signed over his power of attorney to me, which meant I had access to his various accounts so that I could pay bills and move money around for investment purposes. Also, when we had to make medical decisions when he couldn't, a power of attorney allowed me to do that as well. So there are two types of powers of attorney—one for property and one for personal care decisions.

"A power of attorney is really important. For example, if David went into a coma, Alice wouldn't be able to get at bank accounts or investments that were not jointly held unless she had David's power of attorney."

"One thing you must remember about powers of attorney," Uncle Wayne explained, "is that a power of attorney for property is valid as soon as it's signed, so you may want to leave the document with a trusted third party, such as your lawyer, with written instructions that it is only to be released under certain circumstances. That would alleviate any concern that the person you've named might go behind your back and dip into your assets. However, most people shouldn't be too worried about that, because anyone who has your designated power of attorney also has a fiduciary responsibility to you, which means that they must act in good faith. Plus, the Office of the Public Guardian and Trustee will hold attorneys and guardians accountable for their actions and can remove them if abuse or mismanagement occurs."

"My boyfriend has mentioned cases where the power of attorney was with the kids, and they turned around and used the power to try to stop their parents from spending their own money because it was the kids' potential inheritance," Sally stated.

"Aha! So this lawyer friend of yours is your boyfriend," commented Mark. "What does he say about the importance of powers of attorney for property and personal care?"

"He says that people with limited intelligence like you shouldn't be allowed to make their own decisions and, therefore, a power of attorney is crucial," Sally joked. "Actually, what he did say is that powers of attorney are fairly complicated, and even though they may look quite simple, you should probably get professional advice."

"And is he visiting you this weekend to drum up business?" Mark asked snidely.

"Even if he is," Uncle Wayne remarked, "he's right about seeking professional advice. I know one of you mentioned those free do-it-yourself kits earlier, but you're dealing with sizeable estates now, and if I were you, I'd see a lawyer to make sure your wills and powers of attorney are properly drawn up. A mistake you make today doing it yourself could cost your family a fortune in the future.

"I would recommend that you pay a ballpark figure of about $800 to $1,200 for a thorough job. I know it sounds like a lot of money, but remember, like everything else in life, you get what you pay for. Also, the more complicated the planning, the more it may cost to have a proper job done.

"I have one further comment on the personal care aspect of all this. If you don't have a valid personal care power of attorney, it can leave your family in a precarious situation. Also, with your power of attorney, you normally name a back-up or alternate, which is very important. The appointment of a guardian can be made by the court, but this is a last step. It's simple and easy to have a power of attorney done, and you can leave very specific instructions, but married couples often give personal care power to the spouse. It makes sense for Jack and Sandra, and for Alice and David, especially since both couples are giving power of attorney for property to the spouse. Just make sure you have a frank discussion soon, before anything happens, about the kind of care you would want."

"Gee, Mark, you mentioned earlier that you'd signed over power of attorney, but you didn't say to whom," Alice said pointedly.

"Yes, Alice," he replied tersely, "it's my ex-wife. And yes, I will be changing it this week."

Sally had been looking pensive through all this. "You know, Uncle Wayne, you've got great advice for the old married fogies, but it's a bit trickier in my case. Not only am I single, but I'm also the only one in the family who doesn't live within easy commuting distance. I was thinking about who I can really trust, and I'm thinking about naming Jack as my power of attorney currently."

"Sounds good, Sally," Uncle Wayne said. "What do you think, Jack?"

"I think if I'm going to be executor for so many people, I had better bone up on exactly what the job entails. I'm doing it now for Dad's estate, but I've been learning as I go along, and I'm not exactly sure what my precise responsibilities are."

"I'd like to know too," Mark added, "because some day, although I hope it's a long way away, I'll have to handle Mom's estate."

"I have a related question," Sally said. "How can you tell if an executor is doing an honest job, and a good one? I mean, we all trust Jack, but how do we know?"

"Good questions," replied Uncle Wayne, "and here's what I think we should do. Since all three of you are on holidays this week, let's schedule an extra session, say on Wednesday? Over cocktails perhaps? We can discuss the responsibilities of an executor, as long as Alice and David don't mind us going ahead without them."

"Fine by me," David answered. "I hate talking about anything to do with death anyway. Alice can catch up the following weekend for both of us."

"Then we're on," said Uncle Wayne. "And next weekend, we continue with estate planning, specifically the use of trusts and ways to minimize estate costs."

"Perfect," Sally said with a smile. "Well, I hate to eat, take advice, and run, but I have to go and pick up my lawyer friend at the marina."

It was still raining, and as we men rode staunchly back home in the tin boat, getting drenched, I summarized the key points from today's meeting in my mind:

1. Everyone should have a will drawn up, as well as a power of attorney for property and personal care.
2. You should consider factors of trust, ability, financial knowledge, and sometimes even geographical proximity when choosing your executor and designating your power of attorney.
3. A power of attorney for property comes into effect as soon as it is signed.
4. A power of attorney for personal care will not come into effect until or unless you become incapable of making your own decisions.
5. You should review the contents of your will and power of attorney on an annual basis and every time your circumstances change significantly, such as a divorce or birth of a child.
6. Create a digital estate plan.
7. Consult a lawyer and be prepared to spend enough money to ensure the job is done properly and thoroughly.
8. It's important to name trustees and guardians for your children in your will.

   • Consider a professional trustee for your trusts.

9. Spouses might give one another power of attorney for property and personal care to ensure that the spouse has access to all financial assets and can implement your expressed wishes for personal care.
10. It's important to have a frank discussion now with the person who holds your power of attorney for personal care about your specific wishes should you become incapacitated.
11. Introduce your power of attorney for property and your executor to your certified financial planner.

Chapter 7

SO, YOU'RE AN EXECUTOR—WHAT ARE YOUR DUTIES AND LIABILITIES?

The first three days of our vacation were perfect. The temperature was near thirty degrees with just enough of a breeze for windsurfing. The kids were behaving, and all seemed right with the world.

Sally was at the cottage this week too but was staying up in the cabin to try to keep her sanity. She wasn't used to having kids like Connor and Paige running around all over the place.

Mark was staying up for the week with his mom at their cottage, supposedly to help with some odd jobs around the place, but we hadn't heard the banging of his hammer much during those first few days.

When it was time for Uncle Wayne's session on Wednesday, I decided to head over on my windsurfer. Sally took our tin boat and picked up Mark on the way. Sandra stayed behind, happy to get a little time to herself on the deck while Connor and Paige were taking their afternoon naps.

As I tried to land over at Uncle Wayne's, I was going a bit too fast and crashed into the dock with a loud thud. From the deck up above I heard Mark yell, "Great landing, Jack. Do you think you could teach me how to do that?"

"Sure," I shot back. "Right after I teach you how to putt!" If Uncle Wayne hadn't been there, I believe I might have heard an expletive or two in response.

Fortunately, I hadn't gotten wet, and as I climbed up the stairs, I saw Sally, Mark, and Uncle Wayne sipping pina coladas on the sundeck.

"Don't be shy, Jack, yours is in the kitchen," quipped Uncle Wayne.

After I poured my drink and sat down, Sally brought me up to speed. "We were just talking about being an executor. Since you're my brother, I've taken for granted that you're doing a good job, Jack, but in all honesty, I don't even know what it involves."

"Well, for starters," I told her, "I was spending a lot of time, probably three or four hours a week, on various things like meeting with lawyers, the banks, and financial advisors, and also paying the bills, changing the contact for insurance policies for all property, claiming Dad's life insurance, and sorting out the annuity policy and applying for Dad's Canada Pension Plan entitlement. I also had to send documents to the government, and ..."

"Gee, it seems like a big job," Mark commented.

"Yes, I'd say so."

Uncle Wayne jumped in and added, "That's why it's so important to select your executor carefully. Besides a lot of time and effort, it requires some capabilities. I would say the biggest burden is living up to the trust put in you by the person who named you executor. You only have one chance to do a good job."

"Is it a burden, Jack?" asked Sally.

"I think Uncle Wayne hit it on the nose. I want to do a good job, because if I mess up, not only will I have let Dad down, but also you, and David, and all our kids. It's quite a responsibility to handle all those assets, which can run in the hundreds of thousands of dollars, when you're only used to handling your own monthly bills.

"Fortunately, our family has always got along pretty well. There have been no major disagreements so far regarding any of the terms of Dad's will. He divided everything equally, which is how he treated us all his life. As for Dad's personal belongings, well, we haven't divided those up yet, but I think we can manage that by seeing who wants what, and if necessary, drawing straws. We were also lucky that Dad didn't have a rare painting or coin collection, as I've heard of families fighting over who may get a personal item that's worth a lot of money, and the executor has to act as a referee!"

Sally commented, "Dad did a good job in communicating his wishes to us, and it has been really helpful that you've kept us in the loop. As with many things in life, a lack of communication can create problems."

"Thanks, Sally, the only thing that bothers me is that I'm constantly reminded of Dad's death whenever I have to pay one of the bills or meet with his accountant, stuff like that."

Sally's eyes got a bit misty. "I hadn't thought of that."

Mark took that as a cue to change the subject. "What's happening with the cottage?"

"It's part of the overall estate," I said, "and I think Dad did the right thing by not leaving it specifically to any one of us. Whoever really wants it and can afford it can buy it from the estate at market value. If it had been left to one of us kids, a conflict might occur if one of the others became jealous because they wanted the cottage. In addition, the child who received the cottage might not be able to afford the upkeep, or it might not fit into their long-term plans. Anyway, the cottage is up for sale, and we'll divide the proceeds evenly. In the meantime, we've split up the weeks of the summer, and everyone gets some personal time there until it's sold."

Sally was still thinking about an executor's duties. "I didn't realize how tough this could be for you, Jack. I know we don't get along perfectly all the time, but can you imagine how you'd feel if there was a real family dispute, and you were stuck in the middle?"

"There's another very real burden in all this that Jack hasn't mentioned," said Uncle Wayne. "As executor, he is personally liable for the consequences of every decision he makes, such as a mistake in the amount of estate taxes paid."

"Personally liable? Unbelievable," Mark said. "Let's say there's a family feud underway. Could a person turn down the job, even if they've been named executor in a will?"

"Yes, you can," Uncle Wayne told us, "but in many cases, a family feud won't start until after the mother or father dies. There may be jealousy over the terms of the will, or someone may go into a parent's house and cart away the personal items of greatest value, whether financial or sentimental. It's not unusual for disputes like that to crop up. A lot of people react strangely to the idea of getting money, or not getting money that they believe is rightfully theirs. I've seen this happen first-hand with some of my friends' children. If kids don't get along when the parents are alive, they normally won't get along any better when the parents are gone. There's a reason they're called adult children.

"If an executor is worried about the job because of family conflicts, or it's too big of a job for them to handle, they could outsource the role and hire a trust company to assist with the duties. This would add a layer of protection for the executor. If an executor is really, really worried, they could refuse the position before they begin to act, or if they have started to act and have second thoughts, they could resign. This is complicated, so you'd have to review with their lawyer immediately.

"If the beneficiaries are concerned about what the executor has done, they can approach the courts for a procedure called 'passing of accounts,' where the executor can be required to provide a full accounting of all the transactions that have taken place. As a last step, if the beneficiaries believe that the executor is not doing the job properly, they can approach the courts to have the executor replaced. This can be costly and requires a great deal of evidence; however, any costs could be recoverable if they win. As Sally mentioned wisely, ongoing communication is required to hopefully avoid conflicts."

"That sounds like a real mess, Uncle Wayne. I'm glad you all get along most of the time. I'm going to be the executor of my mom's will, many years from now, knock wood," Mark said. "As her only child, I don't exactly expect a family feud, but I'd like to know what my primary duties will be. Could you summarize them?"

"Sure thing. Basically, here's what you've got to do:

1. Locate and review the will.
2. Notify the beneficiaries and provide them a copy of the will.
3. Plan the funeral.
4. Become familiar with the assets of the estate.
5. Protect the estate by making sure the assets, including home, cars, and cottage, are still insured.

   • Notify all the insurance companies and obtain a vacancy permit (insurance for vacant property), as insurance on a vacant property may terminate after a specific number of days.
   • Arrange property checks as required in the policies on vacant property to keep insurance in effect.

6. Obtain help from lawyers and accountants.
7. Locate all the assets and ensure they are properly valued and/ or appraised as required (for the Estate Information Review in Ontario).
8. Turn off the access to all online accounts to prevent identity theft.
9. Meet with the family to discuss the terms of the will.
10. Have the will probated.
11. Pay all creditors.
12. Keep good records.
13. Settle all taxes.
14. Distribute the assets according to the terms of the will."

I nodded to Uncle Wayne and said, "That pretty well sums up the way I'm going at things. The job was made easier because, fortunately, Dad was really organized. He would do an annual review with me, which felt weird at the time, but it was important for me to know where all the assets were, and who his lawyer was, as well as his financial planner and his accountant. He wrote everything down, including his bank account numbers and insurance policies, and he had a digital estate plan with passwords as well. A friend of mine recommended that I close down all the online accounts, as the incidents of identity theft when accounts are left dormant are tremendous. Also, if that information is scattered about, it could take months or even years to find all the assets of an estate."

"I guess I'd better go over all that stuff with Mom," Mark said, "although I don't look forward to talking with her about her death. Can we go back to this liability thing for a minute? I wouldn't mind hearing more about the kinds of things or decisions that could leave an executor liable."

"You'd be held liable if there is contention over any of the estate assets," Uncle Wayne answered. "For example, there could be a dispute over the price received on the sale of certain assets if one of the beneficiaries felt the price was too low. And here's a biggie— if the executor has distributed the assets before receiving the final clearance certificate from Canadian Revenue Agency, the executor is responsible for any shortfall and must personally come up with the money to pay any taxes due from the estate. There's also something called the 'executor's year,' in which the executor has a year to wind up the estate, in most circumstances, and could owe the beneficiaries interest if it takes longer or if they're dragging their feet."

"Wow, that wouldn't be good. Why would anyone distribute the estate before the final clearance?" Sally asked in a bewildered tone.

"Pressure from the heirs," I responded, "who either want or need the money right away."

Sally had another question. "How could you reduce the potential liability and conflict between the executor and the beneficiaries?"

Uncle Wayne thought for a moment and then answered. "I think the best way is to keep good, clear records of where the money is and what it's being spent on. It's a good idea to send written updates to the beneficiaries about what you're doing. Also, it's very important, not to mention smart, to use professional help from lawyers and accountants to do the taxes and probate the will. This will help to reduce your liability as well, by transferring it to the professionals."

"Speaking of taxes, how many returns have you had to do for Dad's estate?" Sally wondered.

"Too many," I said. "The first was Dad's final personal income tax return right up until the date of his death. Now I've got to file an annual return for the estate itself from the date of death until the final distribution of all assets, and that could be several years if the cottage doesn't sell right away. Also, Dad had set up some trusts for the grandchildren, so tax returns have to be done for those too. I also have to apply for the clearance certificate from the CRA."

"No wonder you need an accountant and lawyer," Mark added. "That's a lot of detailed paperwork."

"I can't over-state the importance of getting professional help and keeping good records," Uncle Wayne said. "Being an executor is a very difficult and time-consuming role that carries a great deal of responsibility and liability. You must take great care both in being one and in choosing one for your own estate."

And with that, Uncle Wayne waved his empty pina colada glass in the air. "Time to make another batch, my dear Sally. We'll discuss whether or not, as a beneficiary of your father's estate, you should trust the executor, even if he is your brother!"

SHOULD A BENEFICIARY TRUST THE EXECUTOR?

When we'd all settled back again with fresh drinks on Uncle Wayne's deck, he turned to me with a mischievous smile and asked, "Jack, if you were an unscrupulous executor, what could you do?"

"For starters," I answered, "I could go to the bank and write myself a cheque for the full estate account."

Sally's mouth dropped about a foot. "Do you mean you could legally liquidate everything and write yourself a cheque without us knowing?"

"Who said anything about it being legal? Of course it's not, but the money could all disappear pretty quickly, and me with it! If you're worried," I added, "I suppose I could be bonded by an insurance company."

"That won't be necessary," Sally replied. "Just give me your first-born child until this is all settled."

"I have a serious question," Mark said. "What could we do if we think we're entitled to an inheritance from someone's will, but we don't know for sure?"

"That's easy enough," Uncle Wayne answered. "Ask for a copy of the will."

"What if the executor won't give you one, or just says you aren't a beneficiary?" Mark countered.

"Once the will is probated, it becomes part of the public record, and you can obtain a copy at the court registry office in the county where the person died."

I thought back over my own experience and added, "I'd recommend that any executor give copies of the will to all beneficiaries to avoid confusion and bad feelings."

"Makes sense," Uncle Wayne agreed. "And if you think you might be named in a will, be sure not to sign any form or document without understanding exactly what it means.

"I think the odds on whether or not an executor deserves your trust improve drastically if he or she gives the beneficiaries regular updates that account for the movement of all money into and out of the estate, whether it's for expenses, investments, professional fees, or sums distributed to beneficiaries."

"So," said Sally, "in other words, if the executor seems too quiet about what's going on, or fails to respond to your questions, it could be a sign that you've got a problem. Are there other major concerns to watch out for?"

Uncle Wayne sipped his drink and looked over at me once again before he answered. "I would watch out if the executor was also a beneficiary ... nothing personal, Jack. Also, there could be potential trouble and pressure applied if beneficiaries are competing over an asset. For example, if Jack wanted the cottage, he could turn down all offers to buy it without anyone else knowing it and eventually buy it himself at a low price after a few summers"

"I could see where that could be a problem in some families," Sally commented.

Mark got back into the discussion by asking about executor's fees. He wanted to know how much executors can charge, and whether or not executors who are family members and beneficiaries themselves usually forego the fees.

"Well," Uncle Wayne replied, "executor's fees are a fuzzy subject. In Ontario, they're usually between 3% and 5% of the estate value, and it's not unusual for professional executors, such as trust companies, to charge top-of-the-line fees. However, executors who are also beneficiaries often will do the job at minimal or no cost."

Sally intervened and asked, "Why would you do it for no fees, Jack?"

I responded to her. "There are a couple of reasons. When you receive an inheritance, it's tax free, but executor fees are considered earned income, so it's taxable. But the main reason is if I took a fee of 5%, it could be around $20,000 or more, which is a lot of money, so the other beneficiaries may be envious or jealous."

"Well, what can people do if there's a conflict over executor fees?" Mark asked.

I jumped in to answer. "If you think the fees are too high, you can challenge them in the Superior Court of Justice. They'll have final say on the amount that can be charged. The other provinces all have similar courts; however, they may refer to them by a different name. Also, keep your eyes peeled to make sure the executor doesn't prepay his own fees before distributing the estate."

They all looked at me wide-eyed. "I already ran some of these questions past our lawyer," I explained.

"Are there any other fees we have to watch out for?" Sally asked as she looked at Uncle Wayne.

"If a trust is set up, the trustee fees are usually two-fifths of 1% of the total value of the trust for care and maintenance, and additional fees of up to 2.5% of the capital receipts and disbursements, as well as up to 2.5% of the income receipts and disbursements. If you are going to use a professional trustee, they all have a compensation agreement you can review ahead of time."

"Well, Uncle Wayne, is there anything else we should watch out for?" Mark asked as he drained the last of his pina colada.

"I think that's about it," he answered. "Who wants to take a crack at summarizing the key details for us?"

I said I would try:

1. "Being an executor is a tough job because of the burden of living up to the trust placed in you by the person who gave you the job. It also takes up a lot of time and carries a large amount of personal liability for decisions made.

2. The main job is to manage the estate according to the terms of the will, but this includes making many decisions.

3. The basic duties are:

   - locate and review the will;
   - notify the beneficiaries and provide them a copy of the will;
   - plan the funeral;
   - become familiar with the assets of the estate;
   - protect the estate by making sure the assets, including home, cars, and cottage, are still insured;
   - notify all the insurance companies and consider obtaining a vacancy permit (special insurance for vacant property), as insurance on a vacant property may terminate after a specific number of days;
   - arrange property checks on vacant property to keep property insurance in effect;
   - obtain help from lawyers and accountants;
   - locate all the assets and ensure they are properly valued and/or appraised as required (for the Estate Information Review in Ontario);
   - turn off the access to all online accounts to prevent identity theft;
   - meet with the family to discuss the terms and conditions of the will;
   - have the will probated;
   - pay all creditors;
   - keep good records;
   - settle all taxes; and
   - distribute the assets according to the terms of the will.

4. An executor needs professional assistance from a lawyer and accountant.
5. An executor can build trust with the beneficiaries by:

   - giving a copy of the will to each beneficiary (This is required if the will is probated.);
   - maintaining good records of all transactions;
   - sending regular written updates to beneficiaries; and
   - staying in contact and answering all questions promptly.

6. A beneficiary should be concerned if an executor:

   - refuses to provide a copy of the will (as required);
   - does not send regular updates;
   - ignores your questions or ducks your emails and telephone calls; and
   - is unusually quiet.

7. It is in a beneficiary's best interest to:

   - monitor executor fees and challenge them if they seem too high, and
   - watch for double billing by professional executors."

"That's a pretty good summary," Sally said with a smile. "I think we can trust you, Jack. However, if you're thinking of doing anything rotten, just remember that we will hunt you down like a pig."

Chapter 8

WHO ACTUALLY OWNS
THE INHERITANCE?

The rest of the week was a real scorcher. The temperature was still in the mid-thirties, but there was no wind, not even a breeze.

David and Alice were coming up for a week of holidays, so they had planned to get away early on Friday afternoon to beat the traffic. We figured we had lost our babysitters, because Scott and Jan were staying in the city this weekend. They said it was because they were putting in extra time at their summer jobs, but apparently there was also a big party in the works.

When I saw the boat come into the bay, I dashed up to the cottage to get a couple of cold beers for David and Alice. They looked pretty haggard from the heat as they unloaded their gear. David was still wearing his dress pants, so Alice must have picked him up at the office.

"You guys sure picked a good week for your holidays," David said wearily. "The humidity in the city was a killer."

"I know," I replied. "I feel sorry for your poor kids. Imagine being a teenager and having to stay home in this humidity with the run of a big air-conditioned house and nothing to do but party with all your friends." I was trying to get Alice's goat, but it wasn't working.

"You're right, Jack," she said, rolling her eyes. "They've got it as tough as you did when you were sixteen and had to work up here all summer."

"Yeah, it was tough all right," I admitted. "All those parties and no supervision. I remember one time ..." Something in the look on Sandra's face stopped me dead in my tracks.

David started to laugh. "Some code of silence! You keep breaking it on yourself, you big dummy!"

I thought I could save the day by changing the subject, so I turned to David and said, "The Tiger-Cats play the Argos tonight. One of my old college buddy's son has been really playing well lately."

"Jack, Jack, Jack," Alice interjected. "Enough already. We've all had it up to here with your stories about your buddies and the so-called glory days!"

"Well, Alice, at least I had some glory days."

BREAKFAST

With the heat and humidity, Sandra and I woke up feeling groggy, so we decided to shake out the cobwebs with a quick dip. At the dock we saw Aunt Lorraine take the plunge, while Mark waded in step by step. I could never do that. It was like a slow death.

When we went back up, we saw Connor and Paige playing on the porch with Aunt Sally, while David was fiddling with the barbecue.

"I hope Alice is cooking," I said to him, "and by the way, you owe me five bucks. After you went to bed, the Cats kicked a field goal to win as time expired."

"I'll tell you what," David replied, "either I'll pay you and you have to eat my cooking, or I'll try to talk Alice into cooking. If I succeed, you forget about the five bucks. It's your choice."

"You really are a cheap son of a ... oh, good morning, Connor. How's my boy today?"

Mark's sons were up this weekend with their girlfriends again, and they had offered to take Connor and Paige out for a boat ride during our planning session. Mark was delighted. He thought that an hour or two with a couple of kids might provide a good reality check for these young couples. If nothing else, it might put the brakes on all that kissy-face stuff.

They headed over as soon as they saw Uncle Wayne's boat on the way. Alice had cooked (it was worth the five bucks), so David, Mark, and I were cleaning up the dishes. Aunt Lorraine figured she'd go back to her place for a bit of peace and quiet, and Sandra took our kids down to the dock so they could go off with their cousins.

She walked back up with Uncle Wayne, who was his usual boisterous self. "Good morning, campers! Let's get rolling; I have a golf game today."

"Since when don't you have a golf game?" Sally asked.

"Since whenever I'm over here counselling all of you," he said, putting Sally in her place. "For starters today, we're going to talk about who legally owns the inheritance. Then we'll get into estate planning and how to minimize probate fees and taxes using trusts.

"Now, I know this business about who really owns the money is emotionally loaded, but it's something we have to address, given the high incidence of divorce these days."

"Tell me about it," said Mark.

"So here's the big question," Uncle Wayne continued. "If your marriages break up, or if Jack or David were to die, who does the inheritance belong to? Each couple is going to have to think long and hard about this and take some appropriate action after we investigate all sides of the issue."

"David and I will never get divorced," Alice protested.

"But there's more at issue than our own marital status," Mark said. "I plan to leave an inheritance for my boys, and let's say they're married when I die but get divorced later. I'd prefer to go to my grave knowing that the money I leave to my sons will be passed on to my grandchildren, rather than thinking a bundle could go to some ex-wives someday."

"I hope your sons don't follow in your footsteps when it comes to divorce," Alice remarked, "but I see what you mean, and it's close to home. So, Uncle Wayne, what kind of legal rights do Sandra and I have to the money that David and Jack inherited?"

"Well," he answered, "an inheritance or gift given to one spouse by a third party is not considered to be part of his or her family property if received after the date of the marriage, so the other spouse has no claim to it as part of a divorce settlement. The same thing goes for proceeds from life insurance. However, the re-investment income earned from an inheritance, through investments and the like, is considered to be family property, unless the instructions in the will specifically prohibit this."

"Let me see if I get this," said David. "An inheritance or gift, if received after the marriage, is not part of the matrimonial property, but the income earned on the capital over time is. And the only way to get around it would be for someone like Dad to have specified in his will that the income earned from the inheritance is not to become family property, and this is normally a standard clause in professional wills."

"That pretty well sums it up," said Uncle Wayne.

"And also," continued Alice, "when Mark gets around to changing his will, he should insert a clause stating that any income earned on the inheritance he leaves to each of his sons is for their use only."

"I guess we should all put that kind of condition in our wills," I added. "But what happens in a case like mine and Sandra's, where we've used the inheritance for our mutual benefit? As you know, we've paid off our mortgage and have topped up our RRSPs. How does the inheritance stay separate under those circumstances?"

"Let me try to answer that," said Sally. "I had a call from my lawyer friend this week. He said that once you've started using the money for the benefit of both partners, such as paying off the mortgage or purchasing a matrimonial home, then it's pretty much considered family property, and the value of the joint benefit would be split 50/50 in a divorce. If the spouse who originally inherited the money wants to prevent this, they could have a marriage contract signed, and/or he or she could try to keep the inheritance in his or her own name and segregated from any other assets, especially assets owned jointly."

"But Uncle Wayne has been advising us all summer to do exactly those things," I complained. "And now you're telling me that by doing what makes the most financial sense, I've made it possible for Sandra to take half of the money from Dad's will with her if she decides to leave me! Great. Is there any way to ensure that the inheritance will go to Connor and Paige some day? Frankly, if Sandra does leave me for some young stud, I don't want her to have enough money to set up house-keeping in some Mediterranean villa!"

"The chances of my leaving you would go down considerably if you'd stop talking about your past moonlight cruises," Sandra joked.

At least I think she was joking.

"But seriously," she continued, "I'm sure we've done the right thing by taking Uncle Wayne's advice to heart. It wouldn't have made sense to keep paying interest on a mortgage while we were sitting on a substantial amount of cash. And there must be some way to make sure Connor and Paige get the full benefit of the money left to you by your dad."

Uncle Wayne watched to see if anyone would step forward with a proposal, and sure enough, Alice did.

"How's this for a solution?" she wondered. "Since much of the inheritance, in Jack's case, was used for the house, couldn't Jack and Sandra change the ownership papers? If they became tenants-in-common rather than joint tenants, and if Sandra and Jack signed a marital agreement in which Sandra agreed that she was only entitled to 25% of the house, for example, then Jack could make sure he could get his money out if they ever divorced, and leave his portion to the kids in his will. They could also make sure the money used to top up the RRSPs would go to the kids if Jack died by naming the kids as the beneficiaries."

"That's one way they could go at it," Uncle Wayne said thoughtfully, "but it could get very complicated if Jack did die young. For example, would Sandra have to sell the house to make sure that the kids get the full value of Jack's portion? And would selling the house be in the best interest of the kids? As for the RRSPs, your proposal may not be tax effective. When children over the age of eighteen inherit RRSPs, the plans are collapsed, and the entire RRSP amount is taxed as part of the deceased person's income at the date of death, so in Jack's case, half of the money would go to the government."

"Hey," I said, feeling more than a little hurt, "it's bad enough that I'm always the one who has to die. Now you're saying I must die before the kids are eighteen. That's not fair."

"Well," David remarked, "if Jack's going to be selfish and refuse to die young, then we'll have to find another way to protect our inheritances for the eventual use of our kids. What can we do, other than keeping it separate from family property?"

"I think it's safe to say that you and Jack will probably stay married to Alice and Sandra," Uncle Wayne answered, "so your best bet is to follow the strategies we've been discussing this summer. However, there are several things you can do to keep parts of the inheritance out of the realm of family property and make sure that the value is passed on to your children.

1. Keep good records of precisely how the inheritance was utilized.
2. Any investments made directly with capital from the inheritance should be in Jack's or David's name only. We discussed earlier that the spouse in the lower tax bracket should make the monthly investments, but due to the attribution rules, this only works when investing money earned from income when both people work, not a lump sum that belongs to one spouse. However, both David and Jack could create spousal trusts in their wills so that Sandra and Alice could use the income from the investments for living expenses, while the principal itself is willed to the kids when Alice and Sandra die. I'll go into more detail on trusts a bit later.
3. You can earmark some of the money as a gift you give to the kids now, in trust.
4. You could add up all the money from the inheritance that was used to pay off the mortgage or other debts, or for RRSPs or anything else, and take out a permanent life insurance policy on David or Jack for that amount, with the kids named as the beneficiaries.

"For example, if Jack has spent $100,000 of his inheritance to pay off the old mortgage and top up RRSPs, plus another $50,000 on a new house, he would get a permanent life insurance contract worth $150,000, with Connor and Paige as the beneficiaries. You should check that the structure of the contract lets you pay off and own the policy in about twenty years, and that the money will grow with inflation over that period of time. In addition, you might want to consider having the kids actually 'own' the policy as well as being the beneficiaries. This would ensure that in the divorce scenario we discussed, Jack or David wouldn't be forced to pay money to Sandra or Alice based on the cash surrender value of the insurance policy. If the kids are going to own the policy, watch out for the attribution rules, as they tend to get you every time.

"If you follow these steps, you can be sure that the money your dad left will eventually go to his grandchildren, which I'm sure is what he would have wanted."

"I understand the logic behind all this," Sandra said, "but Jack and I will never get divorced. If Jack dies first, I'll leave everything to Connor and Paige anyway, so why should we spend money on life insurance?"

"The odds are good that you won't get divorced," Uncle Wayne agreed, "but if Jack dies tomorrow, I think the odds are just as good that you'd eventually remarry. And if the inheritance was in your hands at that point, it could become part of the family property of that marriage. And suppose you had more children? It's entirely possible that Connor and Paige might see only 25% of their granddad's money. However, if you act now to protect the value of the inheritance with life insurance, you will guarantee that the money goes to them, and the whole process is much cleaner."

"And since we're all saving money by having paid off our debts," Alice added, "the insurance premiums won't be a financial burden."

"I kind of like this plan," admitted David. "It combines the best of both worlds. We can structure our current finances to take advantage of the inheritance and still ensure that an amount equivalent to the original capital is passed on to our children, regardless of what happens in our lives."

"I agree," Sandra nodded, "and Jack, I'm sure your dad would approve as well."

"It's not that I feel left out or anything, but what about Sally and me?" Mark asked. "I'm not planning on getting married again, but heck, you never know. And Sal's bound to tie the knot someday. Should we be taking any special steps to protect our inheritance?"

"I asked my lawyer friend the very same question," Sally said. "He advised that I insist on a domestic or marriage contract that excludes all prior assets from becoming family property if I ever decide to marry. I reacted by saying it would feel awkward and that a prospective spouse might find it pretty insulting, but he said I'd be surprised at how many people sign contracts like that these days. He also said it helps if you explain that you're safeguarding the inheritance for the next generation."

"You're getting good at this," praised Mark. "I suppose we could also make use of permanent life insurance to be certain that the entire value of the inheritance is passed on to our kids too."

"A few weeks back you told us that term insurance is cheaper," I said to Uncle Wayne, "and I just bought a bunch of it. Now you're recommending permanent life insurance. Please don't tell me I did the wrong thing again!"

"Relax, Jack, and remember what each type of insurance is for. Term insurance is cheaper for the ten to twenty-year period when you want to provide enough capital so that the income from investments would support your dependents if you died. You'll need less of this insurance as your other assets appreciate over time, plus the need will disappear altogether at the end of twenty years because Sandra and the kids will be capable of supporting themselves.

"However, the need to protect the value of your inheritance so that it passes on to your kids is an ongoing requirement. It doesn't end after ten or even twenty years, so you want an insurance policy that builds value and keeps pace with inflation. You can't get that with term insurance, but you can with permanent life if the contract is structured properly.

"And now, if there are no more questions about this, I'd like to take a break. Let's get some more coffee before we finish off estate planning."

"I do have a question," Alice said. "Since he can't even get a date, what makes Mark think he has even a remote chance of ever getting married again?"

Chapter 9

PROBATE, TRUSTS, AND ESTATE TAX MINIMIZING STRATEGIES

"This is great coffee, Sandra," said Uncle Wayne. "I wish you could talk your Aunt Jen into buying the good stuff. She always gets coffee on sale, and it's so weak that I end up needing a whole pot just to get my heart started most mornings. Oh well, let's get back to work.

"I believe we were about to go over information about trusts and some methods you could use to minimize probate fees. So, Alice, has your research taken you down either of these paths yet?"

"Actually, it has," she said with pride. "And from what I can see, there are four major categories of asset transfers, including:

1. gifts, like the lump sum Aunt Lorraine is giving to Mark;
2. non-probatable assets, which pass directly upon a person's death to a beneficiary without having been designated in a will;

3. probatable assets, which are transferred through a will and are, therefore, subject to probate and executor fees; and

4. trusts.

"There are a few different types of trusts, and Uncle Wayne's going to have to help me explain them, because I don't completely understand them. However, what I do understand is that whenever possible, we'll want to transfer assets outside of our wills so that our estates will pay the minimum amount in probate and executor fees."

"I'll second that," I nodded. "Probate fees, or estate administration tax, starting January 2020 in Ontario, is 1.5% of the value of the estate over $50,000."

"Let's not get too far ahead of ourselves," Uncle Wayne said. "I want to go back and look at the pros and cons of each of these methods of transferring assets, starting with gifts.

"But first, there can be some advantages to probate, such as:

- It can protect the executor from claims by the beneficiaries and/ or third parties.
- It can offer some protection from claims against the estate, as there is a specific time frame for claims when a will is probated.
- It may be easier for estate administration by the executor.
- In some cases, it may make it easier to allocate the estate on an after-tax basis to the beneficiaries as intended in the overall estate plan.

"So with any of the strategies, they must be reviewed carefully with your lawyer, accountant, and financial advisor to make sure it makes sense and accomplishes what you intended. You must be concerned about unintended results, which means attempting to save on probate fees that cause other problems."

"What's an example of unintended results?" Alice asked.

"I thank I can answer that," Sally said as she took a sip of her drink. "My lawyer friend mentioned that while you want to minimize probate and estate fees, you have to be careful of unintended circumstances, as Uncle Wayne said. For example, he has seen that some people put their homes in joint ownership with their adult children to avoid probate fees, but this can cause problems. Since the child then owns part of the home, the child's creditors could have access to the property, and the child may also end up with two homes, and only one can be a principal residence, which could cause tax problems."

"Very good point, Sally. This is why you have to include your lawyer and accountant when making and implementing an estate plan," Uncle Wayne said with a smile.

"The transfer of Aunt Lorraine's gift to Mark is tax-free to him and to Aunt Lorraine, because Mark is over the age of eighteen. The only real tax concern is that Aunt Lorraine could have some capital gains on her hands if she had to sell assets that had appreciated in value in order to get the cash to give to Mark. Of course, Mark is ultimately responsible for taxes on income he earns by investing the gift.

"We had also talked about the family cottage with Aunt Lorraine, and if she was to gift the cottage to Mark today, it would avoid the probate fees; however, she would have to pay tax today on the gain between the fair market value of the cottage and the tax cost base. This could be very expensive, since she has had the cottage for over fifty years. To help reduce taxation in the future, she has kept track of the capital improvements, like your new deck, as they increase the tax cost base, and she did bump up the cost base in 1994, as allowable by the CRA back then.

"What she could also do is transfer the cottage into a trust for Mark. The transfer would be tax-free today, but the tax would have to be paid on her death. However, since the property is in a trust, there would be no probate fees, as it passes directly to him. We will review this a bit later.

"Now, getting back to the gifts. The rules for gifts change when the person getting the gift is under the age of eighteen, a minor. In that case, any income earned by investing the gift money is attributed back to the person who gave the gift. For example, if Jack gives money to Connor and Paige, then any investment income from that gift, such as interest or dividends, is still counted as part of Jack's income, and he pays the tax bill. If the investment income earned is capital gains, it's then taxed in the children's hands. However, and here's where it gets really complicated, income earned on the income is not attributed back to Jack.

"The bottom line here is that gifts are more advantageous as a method of transferring assets if you give the money to someone over the age of eighteen or, if the person is under the age of eighteen, the gift is invested in an investment that generates capital gains, such as stocks or an equity mutual fund."

"I think I followed that all right," David commented. "Now, what about non-probatable assets? What are those?"

"I'm glad you asked," said Alice, beating Uncle Wayne to the punch. "Non-probatable assets are assets that are transferred to a beneficiary outside of a will. For example, if spouses own a house together as joint tenants, then one's share passes directly to the other if either die. That means the value of the share in the house doesn't have to go through probate, so no probate or executor fees are paid. Now, with RRSPs ..."

"Hold it a minute," Uncle Wayne interrupted. "You should all know that the same thing applies to bank accounts and other investments that are held jointly. If you don't have joint ownership for financial accounts, then a spouse can't get his or her hands on the assets until they go through probate. Sorry, Alice. Carry on."

"Thanks," she said, smiling. "With RRSPs, you can name a beneficiary, and if it's your spouse, the RRSPs can be passed tax-free and outside the will directly into the surviving spouse's RRSP, without being subjected to probate fees.

"If the beneficiaries are the children or grandchildren, under the age of eighteen and financially dependent, the RRSP proceeds either have to be included in the income of the child or grandchildren, or the proceeds can be used to buy an annuity, payable to the age of eighteen only. If this is done, income taxes would be paid on the income as the kids get it."

"Would my kids be classified as dependent?" asked Mark.

"Under your definition, they probably would," laughed Uncle Wayne, "but not according to Revenue Canada. By their rules, a child over the age of eighteen must be either infirm or handicapped in order to be considered dependent. In a case such as this, the RRSP monies left to them could be rolled over into the dependent child's RRSP or RRIF or used to buy an annuity."

"There's more," Alice cautioned. "You should also name someone as direct beneficiary on all life insurance policies, including your group benefits at work. A lot of people name their estate as beneficiary, but then the proceeds must go through probate, and again, the estate pays a fee, and the heirs get less."

Uncle Wayne added, "Some good points, Alice; however, you most likely will not want to name minor children as beneficiaries of life insurance. By naming your estate, the terms and conditions of your will apply, which is what you most likely desire."

"Well," said Sandra, "if we want to reduce potential probate costs, we'll have to make sure our house and bank accounts are held jointly. What's the procedure, Uncle Wayne?"

"You should double check, and while you're at it, make sure you've named beneficiaries in all of your life insurance policies too. By the way, this stuff should all be in your binders."

"I bet that Mark's life insurance policy at work still lists his ex-wife as beneficiary!" Sally said with a devilish grin.

"You would lose that bet. I changed it last week."

"Can we talk about trusts now?" asked Alice. "As I mentioned, I'm not all that clear on the ins and outs, Uncle Wayne."

David thumped the side of his head as though he hadn't heard her correctly. "I can't believe I heard Alice admit twice in one day that she was unsure about something!"

"Ask me twice if I'm sure I married the right guy," she said with a sideways glance, "and you just might witness this phenomenon again."

"So much for marital trust," Uncle Wayne said. "Now, getting back to the topic of monetary trusts. The advantage in setting up a living trust is that the transfer of assets takes place outside of your will and doesn't have to go through probate, so there are no probate fees and no executor fees. In addition, there may be tax savings, depending on the terms of the trust."

I asked Uncle Wayne what the other uses of trusts are, and he explained to us, "Well, in addition to reducing probate tax, trusts can be used for:

- control and protection of minor children and/or special needs dependents;
- protection for family members who are or could be a financial risk;
- allowing you to income split to lower the family tax rate;
- preserving an inheritance within a blended family, where the surviving spouse is provided for during their lifetime, and the remaining assets are passed to the children upon the surviving spouse's death;
- safeguarding and protection from family law or marital claims upon divorce;
- confidentiality;
- holding an important asset such as a cottage or family business; and
- charitable giving.

"This can be really complicated, and you will have to review with your own lawyer and accountant, but we can review the basics."

"Before I learn the best way to structure a trust, I think I need to know exactly what it is and how it's set up in the first place," said David.

"There's no way to put this without using the legal terms," explained Uncle Wayne, "so here goes. A trust is an obligation that binds a person (the trustee) to deal with the property he controls (the trust property) for the benefit of another (the beneficiary) in accordance with the terms indicated by the person who established the trust (the settlor). What makes this confusing sometimes is that the settlor and the trustee can be one and the same. Here, I wrote it down for you," he said, handing each of us a piece of paper.

Trust	—	entity to which property is transferred
Settlor	—	individual who transfers the property to the trust
Trustee	—	person who makes the decision for the trust
Beneficiary	—	person who will benefit from the property

"I hope you're still with me," Uncle Wayne added, "because there's more. A trust can either be an 'inter vivos' trust or a testamentary trust. An inter vivos trust is a transfer made while you are alive, and it can be either revocable, which means you can change it, or irrevocable, which means you can't.

"The taxation of trusts can also be confusing, but you should remember that the income earned by a living trust is taxed at the highest marginal tax rates, with no deductions. However, if the income earned is paid out to the beneficiaries, it's then taxed as the beneficiaries' income, which allows for income splitting, assuming the beneficiary has a lower tax bracket than the person who gave the property.

"With my own estate planning, since I am an old fogey, we're reviewing a specific type of inter vivos trust called a joint partner trust. These types of trusts allow a settlor (me and my beautiful wife) to transfer capital assets to a trust on a tax deferred basis, provided we are both over the age of sixty-five at the time of the transfer. The conditions are that we as settlors must receive the income from the trust and pay tax on it each year. The capital gains tax is deferred until our deaths. Now there are some set up fees and tax returns to file, so we're weighing the pros and cons of perhaps putting the family cottage and some of our investment portfolio into a joint partner trust for our kids. Aunt Lorraine is looking at the similar type of trust for Mark for the cottage as we discussed early, but since she's single, it's called an alter ego trust.

"The other kind of trust, a testamentary trust, is something you set up under the terms of your will. That means the assets will have to go through probate, and the estate will have to pay fees, but at least you maintain some control over how the assets are handled after you're dead.

"If it sounds complicated, believe me, it is. What's important, though, is that you understand the concept of the trust, how it's taxed, and who pays what. That's what your lawyer or accountant is for. Let's take a look at how you can all use these strategies in your individual circumstances.

"Sally, since you're single with no kids, there's really not much you can do to minimize probate and executor fees other than making sure you designate a beneficiary other than your estate on your group life insurance policy at the office. But there's lots you married folks with kids can do, and here's the course of action I'd recommend for David and Alice, and for Jack and Sandra:

1. Make sure the house and bank accounts are joint holdings.
2. Name one another as beneficiary for your RRSPs and TFSAs.
3. Set up a spousal trust for the investments that were made with capital taken directly from the inheritance.
4. Set up a testamentary trust for each child in your will for all remaining assets.
5. Since David and Jack are taking out permanent life insurance to ensure that the original value of their inheritance goes to their kids, name the estate as beneficiary so the terms of the will apply. You could also look at an insurance trust instead of naming the estate, but that can get complicated."

"I think I'm going to need a little help making sense out of those instructions," I confessed.

"No problem," responded Uncle Wayne. "Joint ownership on the house and bank accounts ensures that the holdings pass directly to your spouse, with no probate fees. Same thing for the RRSPs and TFSAs if you name your spouse as beneficiary; however, please review your overall estate plan to make sure that by making your accounts joint, and naming beneficiaries, you don't defeat the purpose of your estate plan to begin with. Mark, you will have to pay attention to this, as this can happen when someone has had a prior marriage or relationship that included children and support payments, and perhaps has made some charitable gifts in their estate plan or has other financial obligations. You have to be very careful and think about the overall estate plan and intentions before changing anything."

"Thanks, Uncle Wayne, I'll remember that," Mark added.

Uncle Wayne continued, "If you set up spousal trusts for the investments you made outside your RRSPs with capital taken directly from your inheritances, then Alice and Sandra can live on the income from the investments, but the capital stays secure and will go to the kids when their mothers eventually die. The other advantage to this arrangement is that the investments transfer into the spousal trusts without requiring your estate to pay capital gains taxes currently. This concept is often referred to as a 'rollover.'"

"Oh," I commented, "so by doing this, we defer capital gains taxes, and we make sure that our inheritance from Dad eventually goes to his grandchildren, but our wives are taken care of for as long they live. Good plan."

David added, "It seems fair."

"I agree," said Alice, looking at Sandra. "After all, it's not our money."

Uncle Wayne continued. "Both of your families have term insurance to provide income for living expenses and childcare if anything should happen to you. To split income, you could name your spouse as the beneficiary for the major portion of the term insurance, but you should also name each of the children directly, with your spouse named as a discretionary trustee. This way, some of the money would go to the children directly in trust, and as discretionary trustee, your spouse will be able to use it for the cost of care and education as necessary. It's tax effective because the income on the funds earned in the trust, if paid out, will be taxed at the children's lower income tax rate. So the same income may be earned, but it's divided among two or three people. This is an effective income splitting strategy. Also, you can designate the age at which the money is to be given to the children. The trust document has to clearly set this out.

"Now, we hate to even think about this, but setting up a testamentary trust in your wills for each of your children covers the bases to protect and help them. As I mentioned earlier, the assets in a testamentary trust do have to go through probate, but this setup allows tax splitting of the income from the assets in the trusts, and it also lets you determine when the children will gain control of the assets.

"For example, as we discussed a few weeks ago, you may want the trustee to withdraw funds for normal expenses, such as the cost of university, but you probably don't want your kids to get their hands on their entire inheritance at a young age."

"We've already made provisions in our wills for paying the cost of university for our kids," Sandra remarked. "What I'd like to know is whether there's any way to set aside money for their education now that could also give us a tax break."

"I've got some information on that," David responded.

I guess we all looked pretty stunned.

"Knock it off. Alice doesn't have a monopoly on research. Anyway, here's the scoop. There's a federal program out there called a Registered Education Savings Plan (RESP), and there are two basic types.

"The first type is where you have your own self-directed education trust plan. You would make the investment decisions (such as a mutual fund) and name a beneficiary, which can be changed if it is a blood relative. You can contribute up to $2,500 per year, or a lifetime total of $50,000, for each child. There's no immediate tax benefit or deduction like an RRSP when you make the contribution, but the money in the plan can grow tax-free, and you get a 20% grant on the contributions, to a maximum of $7,200 lifetime. There are also some other benefits, depending on your family income.

"So within the plan, you'll have your contributions, the grant, and growth. When the grant and growth are taken out, it's taxed in the hands of the child, which is normally in a lower tax bracket. Contributions are removed with no tax. If one child doesn't use the RESP, another child can use it. In the worst case scenario, if no one can use the RESP for post-secondary school, you would get your contributions back tax-free. You have to pay back the grants, and you have to pay tax on the growth when redeemed, or rollover tax-free to your RRSP if you have room.

"The other type of plan is a single plan with a multitude of subscribers, often called a scholarship trust. In this plan, those who don't go to university lose their contributions and pay for those who do, so I would not recommend using these types of plans."

Uncle Wayne added, "With an RESP, if you and your wonderful spouses are joint subscribers and anything happens to one of you, the other can take over. If there's only one subscriber, you may want to name a successor subscriber in your will so that the RESP can continue and won't be collapsed in the estate."

Mark said, "My head's starting to spin, and you haven't got around to me yet! What do you think I should be doing?"

"Since your kids are past eighteen, I'd recommend that you set up a testamentary trust in your will that would specify the ages at which your kids gain control of their inheritance, and instruct the trustee when and how to dole out money for their school and living expenses in the meantime. Your sons are quite responsible, but I still recommend that you not leave them their entire inheritance all at once, in case they blow it.

"Now, since you're no longer married, you may want to consider a permanent life insurance policy, with your sons as beneficiaries, that will cover any capital gains taxes on your investments and on your business when you die, plus about half the value of your RRSPs. Remember, your RRSPs will be taxed near the 50% level when you die. The permanent life policy will ensure that the true value of your estate will go to your kids, assuming that's what you want."

"I just thought of something," Sally said, jumping back into the discussion with vigour. "If you use investment products offered by life insurance companies, you can name a beneficiary directly, so the investments remain separate from your estate and can pass to beneficiaries without going through probate. You can save a bundle, and this applies to both RRSPs and other investments as well.

"Plus, if you've got your money in segregated funds instead of mutual funds, then the insurance companies will guarantee that your beneficiaries receive either the market value of your investments or up to 100% of the original principal you invested, depending on which company you're with."

"Another date with your friend from the insurance business?" Mark asked.

"Actually, I'm dating his roommate, a jazz trombonist. Shall we talk about your love life now?"

"Okay, you two, I've heard all I want to hear about dating," warned Uncle Wayne. "Good heavens, my last date was fifty years ago, but that's another story. Anyhow, Sally's right about insurance company products. Just remember, do your homework to make sure the company's on solid ground.

"And although we've been over this before, it bears repeating. As a business owner, Mark may find segregated funds to be particularly attractive because they're creditor-proof, so if he's sued, a third party can't get at his investments. Also, Mark, with your business assets, you can have a secondary will for those specifically, and it will bypass probate."

"That's a good point," Mark agreed.

"Well," said Uncle Wayne, "I haven't got much to add on the subject of trusts and probate fees, unless you've got some more questions."

"I remember you gave us criteria for selecting an executor," Sandra mentioned, "and I would imagine you want us to use the same guidelines in choosing a trustee. What's it going to cost us to set up a trust?"

"I am glad you brought this up," he answered, "because there's no point in trying to cut corners. You need a lawyer familiar with trusts; it will probably cost you a few thousand dollars, and you might as well have the work done in conjunction with your wills and powers of attorney. And yes, Sandra, you must choose your trustees very carefully. After all, they could wind up with your children's futures in their hands."

Uncle Wayne let out a happy sigh and then continued. "I won't be available next weekend, so let's get together on Labour Day weekend for a final session. Our discussions have set out a framework for all of you, but we need to talk about selecting a team of advisors who can guide you when I'm down south playing golf this winter!"

Sandra and Alice said they would prepare a special meal for our last breakfast, and that Uncle Wayne was to bring Aunt Jen along.

Later that night after we put Connor and Paige to bed, Sandra and I each had a glass of wine, hers expensive and white, mine cheap and red. We started to review the main points from the day's dual session, and Sandra opened her laptop and started to make some notes:

1. Inheritances, life insurance proceeds, and gifts belong to the individual and are excluded from the legal definition of family property if received after marriage.

2. The income and growth produced by investments made with the capital from an inheritance, insurance proceeds, or gifts are considered family property unless the will or document

specifically states that the income and growth are for the sole use of the individual.

3. Once you start to comingle the assets by paying off a mortgage or topping up RRSPs and TFSAs, the assets are generally considered to be part of family property.

4. David and Jack could protect the full value of their inheritance for their children by adding up the capital spent on joint assets and then buying a permanent life insurance policy for that amount, with the children named as beneficiaries.

5. Single or divorced people like Sally and Mark should consider insisting on a domestic contact (commonly called a marriage contract) that excludes all prior assets from being part of family property.

6. Probate and estate costs can be minimized by:

- designating specific beneficiaries on life insurance policies and, in some cases, for RRSPs and TFSAs;
- making sure spouses have joint ownership of such assets as houses, bank accounts, and investments so that the assets are transferred outside the will with no probate fees;
- using gifts while alive;
- establishing trusts that can minimize estate costs, since property in an inter vivos trust does not form part of the estate for probate purposes;
- establishing spousal trusts for Sandra and Alice to provide enough income for their living expenses if Jack or David died, while ensuring that the capital is eventually passed on to the children (Spousal trusts also can be used to defer capital gains taxes.);
- if you are over the age of sixty-five, reviewing the potential use of alter ego and joint partner trusts to avoid probate fees.

7. Trusts can be used for:

- control and protection of minor children and/or special needs dependents;
- protection for family members who are or could be a financial risk;
- potentially income splitting to lower the family tax rate;
- preserving an inheritance within a blended family, where the surviving spouse is provided for during their lifetime and the remaining assets are passed to the children upon the surviving spouse's death;
- safeguarding and protection from family law or marital claims upon divorce;
- confidentially;
- holding an important asset such as a cottage or family business;
- charitable giving; and
- reducing probate tax.

8. The funds earmarked for a testamentary trust will be subjected to probate fees but are a useful way to split income by naming the children as beneficiaries, with your spouse as trustee, and usually one or two other trusted individuals, so the income earned will be split among two or three people.

9. An inter vivos trust may not offer immediate tax advantages in relation to current income if the beneficiaries are under the age of eighteen, or if it is your spouse, since any income earned will be taxed in your hands, unless it is capital gains income for the children. But the assets in an inter vivos trust will not go through probate or have any estate costs, so it is a tax effective estate planning tool. It also allows you to maintain control over the assets in the trust.

10. If you use insurance company investment products, such as segregated funds, you can name a beneficiary, and the assets will pass outside the will without any probate or executor fees.

11. Insurance company investment products are also considered to be creditor-proof.

12. If you have an RESP as a sole subscriber, you may want to consider naming a successor subscriber in your will so the RESP will continue.

13. For business owners, the use of a secondary will can avoid probate fees on those assets.

14. Some probate and estate tax minimizing strategies can have unintended consequences, so you will have to review all strategies with your insurance expert, accountant, lawyer, and financial advisor in conjunction with your entire estate plan.

Chapter 10

THE END OF SUMMER

I could hardly believe it was already the Labour Day weekend. We had all arrived at the cottage on Friday night, and this would likely be the last time we'd all be together until Thanksgiving. It was easy to tell that summer was almost over. These days, the temperature went down when the sun did, and we were huddled around the fireplace in our sweaters and sweatpants. We'd all chipped in to get a gift for Uncle Wayne to thank him for his advice and guidance this summer. We'd put Alice in charge, and now we couldn't get her to tell us what she'd bought.

"All summer you wouldn't keep quiet," I teased, "and when we finally want you to talk, you refuse!"

"I'd watch my step if I were you," she countered. "If you're mean to me, I'll make you executor of my estate, now that I know what a difficult job it can be. I kind of like the idea of you sitting in a stuffy office with a calculator for hours on end with my kids constantly nagging you for money."

"Well, Alice, even if you did that to Jack," Sandra said, "I'm sure your instructions would be so clear and well organized that even he could do a good job."

"Oh great," I muttered. "Even when Alice is gone, she'll still be telling me what to do."

"But Jack," said David, defending his wife, "Alice is the one who told you it would be a mistake to let Sandra get away. Remember when you two started dating, and one of your old girlfriends called? You asked Alice for advice, and ..."

"So much for our code of silence!" I said. "Thanks a lot, David. By the way, did you ever tell Alice about that weekend up here with your university pals, when you met those girls who were working at the Delawana Inn? I seem to recall that ..."

"David, I would like to speak with you outside, please," Alice said in a frosty tone.

"Jack, I'm glad it's too cold outside for bugs tonight," said Sandra, shaking her head.

"Why? Do you think Alice will keep him out there a long time?"

"No. I'm glad for your sake. It means you won't get eaten alive tonight when you're sleeping out there in the boat!"

"You guys sure make marriage look mighty attractive," Sally grumbled. "I'm going to bed."

Mark woke us up when he jumped into the water for his usual morning dip before breakfast. It's a good thing too, because we had a full house coming for breakfast, and it was time to get rolling. We sort of ate in shifts, with plates on our laps, because there were thirteen of us: Sally, David, Alice, Scott and Jan, Sandra, Connor and Paige, Mark, Aunt Lorraine, Uncle Wayne, Aunt Jen, and me.

True to their word, Alice and Sandra had prepared a virtual feast, including blueberry pancakes, fresh sticky buns, sausages, back bacon, and scrambled eggs with smoked salmon. I don't know about everyone else, but I had sure gained a few pounds from our breakfast meetings all summer.

Aunt Lorraine and Aunt Jen were just about to leave with all the kids for their usual Saturday trek down to the harbour when Sally asked them to hang around for a few minutes.

"We have a special presentation for Uncle Wayne," she explained as she gestured toward Alice, who was holding an oblong package and wearing a grin from ear to ear.

She handed the box to Uncle Wayne, saying, "We hope you'll enjoy this small token of our appreciation for your patience, good advice, and hard work this summer. You were really terrific, Uncle Wayne. Thank you."

"Hear, hear," we all chimed in as Uncle Wayne opened his present. It was one of the newer state-of-the-art putters, along with a framed picture of all of us taken at the golf tournament. The inscription on the picture read, "Thanks for looking after our interests. With love from the Saturday Strategy Club."

"What a great picture!" beamed Uncle Wayne. "Look at this, Jen. They're all smiling, even Mark, and right after I had cleaned his clock too. Good stuff. We'll put this right over the mantle at our cottage. And tell you what, Mark, you can have my old putter. Thanks, everyone. To tell you the truth, spending that time with you was almost as much fun as golfing."

THE LAST SESSION

"And if everyone but the Saturday Strategy Club will kindly clear out, we can get down to business," he continued with a wink.

"We know," we said in unison. "You have a golf game."

I started the conversation and asked Uncle Wayne, "Do you think it's important to have a family meeting with our beneficiaries, like Dad did with us?"

"Alice has some good insight into this. I know she has had several conversations with her parents. Can you let us know what you spoke about?"

"Well," Alice started, "after our planning sessions with Uncle Wayne this summer, I thought I should bring up the subject with my parents, and we had some great discussions. The three conversations we ended up having were:

1. an estate document conversation,
2. an eldercare conversation, and

113

3. a family legacy conversation."

"So, Alice, was the estate document conversation basically what you had talked about previously, when you had a conversation with your parents to find out who their executor and power of attorney were, the location of all their documents, and an introduction to their financial advisor?" I asked.

"Yes exactly," she answered. "My brother and I sat down with our parents to review their documents, and we met with their financial advisor and had a frank discussion on what they wished to happen and how they wanted to have their finances handled if they were unable to make decisions for themselves. We found this very helpful, and we're going to set another meeting to see if she may be a good fit as our advisor as well.

"The next conversation this led to was an 'eldercare' conversation based on the advice Uncle Wayne had given me. In this conversation, we discussed and made plans with our parents about what they wanted us to do if a potential medical or physical setback occurred as they aged. For example, what would the plan be if:

- they needed some extra help to continue to live at home,
- they decided they had to or simply wanted to move into a retirement home,
- they wished to downsize their current home at some point,
- only one of them needed care in a retirement home, and
- both or only one had to go into a long-term care facility?

"It was good to review this with them ahead of time so that we could discuss some scenarios. Since we've also met with their financial advisor, we know where to go to if we need to model out some of the options."

"That's a great idea," Sandra added. "I don't even know who has my parents' power of attorney; I assume it's my brother and I, but I'm not sure."

Alice took a sip of coffee and continued. "We also had a legacy conversation with my parents, and this is something that I think we should also have with our kids. What do you think, Uncle Wayne?"

"Absolutely a great idea," Uncle Wayne chimed in. "I know you all found it valuable to discuss what your dad's wishes were, especially regarding how the cottage was to be dealt with. I'd recommend it for everyone, as soon as you think the kids are old enough.

"There's one other thing I think all of you may want to do, and that's to write a letter to your future self about eldercare so that you can put your thoughts in place while you're able to. This would be for you to read, and your children as well, when required. We are just drafting our own, and some of the key items are:

- where we want to live,
- our desire to not put the obligation on our children to act as our primary care givers,
- the need to spend our money so that our kids don't have to do stuff for us if we can't live safely at home,
- if we're in a retirement home, and our kids don't recognize us, our desire that they not waste their time visiting us each day."

"I think that would be very helpful," I added.

Uncle Wayne then continued. "Some of the reasons I think that you should all have these conversations with your kids and parents is that it will allow you to:

- share your values with your children;
- let them know what you wish to happen as you age and your parents age;
- reduce confusion, discord, and potential family conflict;
- talk about any concerns you may have; and
- help you to feel in control and let them know that you have a plan.

Some of the potential topics to review could be:

- the values you wish to pass on, and why you are legacy planning;
- who will have a leading role in your planning;
- health care issues, such as the eldercare plan;
- what's important to you in the legacy and wealth transfer;
- why you may be using trusts versus an outright distribution;
- potential controversial issues such as unequal distributions;
- special considerations;
- any charitable giving in your plan;
- your gifting goals while alive;
- your plans for your business, such as Mark has; and
- who your advisors are."

"I'd recommend that you have these discussions with your kids and your parents if possible. It has put my brother and me at ease, as we know where to go to and what to do if something happens to them," Alice said as she started to tear up slightly. "Something that we found out, which we had no idea of prior, was our parents' financial commitment to a few charities that meant a lot to them. It was interesting to see the strategies they used. Our mom had decided to leave her RRIF to her favourite charity, a women's shelter in Hamilton. She did that by naming them as the beneficiary of the plan. Our dad last year had donated some stock he'd owned for a while to his favourite food shelter. Not only was this great for them to do, but it created some tax savings as well. For example, the stock my dad donated had appreciated in value over the years and had a huge taxable capital gain. By donating the stock, he didn't have to pay the tax on the capital gain, and he received a charitable tax credit today.

"By my mom designating the women's shelter as the beneficiary of her RRIF, her estate will then receive a charitable tax credit for her final tax return, which will help offset taxes. Their financial advisor, Joan, helped them with this strategy. She also recommended that when leaving money in your will to a charity, be sure to leave a specific amount rather than a percentage of the estate, as this will help to avoid confusion and potential litigation."

"That's awesome advice," Sandra congratulated her. "Thanks for letting us know."

Alice continued. "There is one other very important conversation that we want to have, and that's a 'next gen financial education conversation' with our kids. From our meetings this summer with Uncle Wayne, we realized that there are many basic financial concepts that we should have known but we didn't. We didn't learn the concepts in high school, and we didn't learn them in university. In thinking about it, Uncle Wayne, this winter you should write a book about financial planning for millennials!"

"That's a great idea. Perhaps I can do that in my spare time down south this winter!" Uncle Wayne then suggested, "I know that most kids will ignore their parents, and I would be happy next summer to arrange a weekly get together for all your kids, plus some of the friends if they want. Since some will be going to university, and some are starting their first full-time jobs, some critical topics could be:

- how to budget for post-secondary school;
- your first job and setting a lifestyle you can afford;
- simple budgeting and cash flow planning;
- understanding how taxes work;
- leasing versus buying a car;
- understanding your employer's benefit package;
- setting up a savings program;
- understanding the impact of interest charged on credit cards;
- the difference between good debt and bad debt;
- types of investments, such as high interest savings accounts, mutual funds, stocks, ETFs, etc.;
- types of savings vehicles, such as TFSAs and RRSPs; and
- the financial impact of life's transitions, such as

  o getting married,
  o buying a home,
  o having children,
  o changing jobs or careers,
  o getting divorced,

o   caring for an elderly parent,

o   safeguarding any inheritance they may receive.

"Also, I think it would be a great idea to have your kids start to work with your financial advisor's company once you find one. The earlier they start, the better.

"Speaking about financial advisors and advice, who feels confident enough after our summer sessions to handle their own finances without any outside help? Hmm. No one? Not even Alice? Good! Because we're talking about your future here, and as the old saying goes, a little bit of knowledge can be a dangerous thing."

David nodded. "Even though your advice has got us thinking in the right directions, there's a lot of detailed work when it comes to developing, implementing, and then monitoring financial plans. The more I learn, the more convinced I am that Alice and I should hire professional help."

"I agree," said Mark. "After a busy day at work, the last thing I want to do is come home and spend all night reviewing my investments and other personal affairs. It's one thing to make overall decisions based on sound financial strategies, but it's quite another to have to monitor movement within your portfolio daily. Phooey on that."

"I'm with you, cousin," Sally said. "To do a proper job, we'd have to keep up with every change in the rules regarding trusts and taxation, as well as track all the trends in both the domestic and international markets."

"We shouldn't even try to do those things on our own," Sandra reasoned. "I look at it this way—we've all had some degree of success in our own jobs, and at least part of that success is due to training and hands-on experience, which fosters an understanding of how our various professions work. It makes perfect sense to me to hire someone who's been trained and successful in the field of financial management to help us with our money plans. I guess it's possible that we could do a good job, but it's just too important to leave to chance."

"You've been quiet, Jack," said Uncle Wayne.

"I think we're all together on this one," I commented. "Your advice has helped us set goals and objectives, and we've even taken some of your recommended actions, such as signing powers of attorney. But now, we're going to need some ongoing guidance. Who do you think we ought to see?"

"Let's first review how financial advisors typically work in Canada. In preparation, I read a report from July 2014 called, "Sound Advice Insights into Canada's Financial Advisor Industry," prepared by PWC for Advocis, the Financial Advisors Association of Canada. The report explains that financial advisors generally work in four broad advisor segments:

1. full-service brokerage
2. branch advice
3. insurance-based
4. financial advisor dealer."

"What does this all mean?" I asked Uncle Wayne.

"Well, it basically describes how they work. Advisors who work at full-service brokerages basically work for one of the big banks, although there are some non-bank owned companies.

"Branch advice advisors are those who work at a deposit-taking institution, such as bank or credit union.

"An insurance-based advisor is contracted with a life insurance company directly, or with a larger group called an MGA, which means Managing General Agent.

"The last main channel, financial advisor dealers, are advisors working outside of a depositing-taking institution."

"What about ROBO advisors?" Sally chimed in. "Some of my friends are using them."

Mark commented, "I've looked into them, and currently it appears they are more about ROBO investments versus financial advice, as they only provide investments, with little or no advice outside of that.

"So if we want to work with a full-service advisor, does it really matter which type of firm they work for?" Mark asked.

"The specific channel is not the most important factor; however, you will want to deal with a firm that is financially strong. I'd suggest that the most important factor would be the specific advisor you decide to work with. You'll want an advisor who provides holistic plan-driven advice, and who puts your interest first.

"There are numerous designations in the financial advisor business, but based on what we've talked about and your need for ongoing support, I'd recommend that you opt for a financial advisor who has obtained the CFP® or CERTIFIED FINANCIAL PLANNER® professional designation, as they are trained in of the following key areas:

1. financial management,
2. retirement and cash-flow strategies,
3. investment management,
4. tax planning,
5. insurance and risk management, and
6. estate planning.

"CERTIFIED FINANCIAL PLANNERS are generalists who can help you develop a full plan and will call on the specialists for help when necessary. Also, in the 2019 spring budget in Ontario, it was proposed to introduce legislation that those who wish to use the financial planner or financial advisor titles have the appropriate credentials."

"I suppose that our financial team should include an accountant, lawyer, and insurance expert in addition to our planner," Sally speculated.

"Yes," Uncle Wayne answered, "and here's an analogy that Jack will like. The financial planner or advisor is sort of like the head coach of a football team; he calls the plays and co-ordinates the actions of the other coaches and players on the team who have the expertise necessary to make the big play.

"When developing financial, estate, and tax plans, you'll want to make sure that your accountant and lawyer agree with what should be done, and that all the appropriate documents are created. For example, will and estate planning has to take into consideration the beneficiary designations on your RRSPs and RRIFs. The CERTIFIED FINANCIAL PLANNER may help you to develop an overall plan, but it has to be implemented and reviewed by your accountant and lawyer."

"I know what makes a coach good, Uncle Wayne," I remarked, "but how do I know whether a financial planner is good? Are there any checklists or criteria available?"

Alice mentioned, "I'm on the FP Canada web site, the organization that looks after the CFP designation in Canada, and they have a bunch of good information about this. I'll send you all the link to their web site, www.fpcanada.ca."

"Why don't we develop our own in addition?" Uncle Wayne asked. "Mark, what would you look for?"

"I think education is important," Mark replied. "I'd want my financial planner or advisor to have a university degree, and preferably a graduate degree, such as a Master of Economics or Business, as well as be a CERTIFIED FINANCIAL PLANNER professional. With so many people advertising their services, why not select someone who's well educated with a demonstrated ability to keep on learning as things change."

"Experience is another important factor," said Alice. "And not just in the financial services industry, but also in the area of wealth management. I'd want someone who's familiar with all the things Uncle Wayne has talked about, and who's worked with people like us before."

"Anything else?" asked Uncle Wayne.

Sandra spoke up. "I want someone who's relatively independent and isn't allied with one particular company, so she would have access to a wide variety of products on the market without harbouring a vested interest."

I told Sandra that I agreed with her, and added, "I think we'd also select someone who has a network of contacts, access to accountants and lawyers who specialize in trusts, and all the executor stuff."

"What have we missed?" Alice asked.

"A couple of points," he answered. "First of all, I would use a financial advisor that specializes with clients who are similar to you. Also, try to get references from the financial advisor's other clients, as well as any accountants or lawyers who may have recommended the financial advisor to their own clients.

"A last point is that it's probably best to choose someone tied to the local area, such as a long-time resident. Reputation is very important to people like that, and they'll probably take great care with your money."

"How do you suggest we find a financial advisor?" asked Sally.

"We've been trying to find one," I mentioned. "First I asked my friends if they would recommend anyone. I then spoke to my accountant and asked her for some recommendations. From the recommendations I did some online research about them, looked at their web site, reviewed if they had written any articles about financial planning, and to see if they worked with a specific type of client, and finally confirmed if they had a CFP designation. From this, I made appointments with three of them and asked them the following questions I found on the FP Canada web site:

- What are your qualifications?
- What experience do you have?
- What services do you offer?
- What's your approach to financial planning?
- Will you be the only person working with me?
- How will I pay for your services?
- How much do you typically charge?
- Who besides me benefits from your recommendations?
- Are you regulated by any organization?
- Can I have it in writing?"

"That's a good list. So how do financial advisors get paid?" asked Sandra.

"Some advisors still earn commissions on the products they recommend and sell, such as mutual funds or insurance. Some charge a flat fee for planning work, and many charge an asset-based fee based on the amount of money you have invested. This fee could either be paid from within the specific investments you own, or deducted from your investment account, or paid from your bank account. Regardless of which way they charge, it's up to you to make sure you fully understand what you're paying and to understand what you're receiving for the fees you pay!"

"So once we hire a financial advisor, what is the process?" asked Sally.

Uncle Wayne took a sip of his coffee and continued. "Normally the ongoing process they would follow would be to

1. find out what your family's dreams, hopes, goals, and desires are;
2. benchmark your current financial reality;
3. co-create the required strategies and plan that will enable you and your family to achieve your dreams, hopes, and desires in the time frame you have selected;
4. execute your specific strategy in the following five key areas:

   a. retirement and cash-flow strategies,
   b. investment management,
   c. tax planning,
   d. insurance and risk management, and
   e. estate planning;

6. use a detailed checklist-driven, step-by-step process to ensure nothing is missed in the execution of your plan; and
7. provide an on-going annual review of all aspects of your strategy and plan to make sure they remain aligned with what your family wishes to accomplish over time."

"That's our Uncle Wayne," I said. "A veritable fountain of knowledge."

"And that, my dear young friends, signals the end of our final meeting of the Saturday Strategy Club. We've covered the basics, and now it's up to each of you to plot your own path and goals based on what's important to you. But remember … to stay on track, an annual review of your goals, strategies, estate plans, and Double Os must be done."

"Thanks again for all of your hard work," I said.

"And thank you all for yours," Uncle Wayne replied. "Sally, David, Jack, I know your dad would be proud of the responsibility you're showing by handling your inheritance in a way that safeguards it for the next generation. Just remember that he had a lot of fun in life, and he'd want you to have some fun with the money too.

"Now, I hope I can count on all of you to help pull my dock out of the water on Thanksgiving. I've got a few other chores lined up too. Sally, why don't you forget the musician and get yourself a handyman for a boyfriend?"

And with that, Uncle Wayne gave us a wink and headed down to the dock. Sandra, Sally, and I saw him off and then joined the others inside, where Alice reviewed Uncle Wayne's approach to handling our sudden wealth. He had talked with us about:

1. what to do first;
2. how to maximize returns and protect our assets in the short term, which debts to pay off, and in what order;
3. investment strategies to allow for both growth and protection of capital;
4. tax strategies to maximize growth of the inheritance;
5. how to develop an effective estate plan;
6. how to select an executor, and whether you should trust an executor;
7. who legally owns an inheritance or gift, and when the assets come to be regarded as family property;
8. strategies to safeguard an inheritance or gift for the next generation;
9. how to use trusts to our best advantage;
10. the four critical conversations everyone should have with their kids and parents:

    • the estate document conversation
    • an eldercare conversation
    • the family legacy conversation
    • the "next gen financial education conversation" with your children;

11. how to assemble a financial team; and
12. an annual review of goals, strategies, estate plans, and Double Os.

THANKSGIVING WEEKEND

The change from Labour Day to Thanksgiving was like the difference between day and night. The leaves had long since peaked, and everything that had once been shiny and green was now dreary and brown. At five degrees, even the water looked darker than usual.

Getting Uncle Wayne's dock out of the water was no picnic, and Sally and Mark made it even worse by starting a splash fight that soaked everyone.

Later, when we were gathered around the fireplace with a bottle of red wine after dinner, Sally wanted to know what we'd all done with our inheritance.

"I thought we covered that last summer," Mark snorted. "Earth to Sally, what planet have you been on?"

"Yeah, yeah. You know what I mean. What specific steps have you taken to implement the strategies Uncle Wayne talked about?"

"Jack and I have been really conscientious," Sandra said with pride. "We've put together a financial team with a planner, an accountant, and a lawyer. In fact, right now our lawyer's in the process of setting up a couple of trusts for the kids. Of course, we told you last summer that we had taken out extra term insurance for income protection, and now Jack's shopping for an additional permanent life policy to guarantee that Connor and Paige receive the full value of the money left behind by their granddad."

"David and I have taken some of those same steps," Alice said, "but we're not rushing into anything. We're still toying with the idea of buying this place, but it looks less likely as time goes on. How about you, Mark?"

"Mom had the proper documents drawn up to ensure that the gift and any income earned on the money she gave me wouldn't become part of family property if I ever marry again. No cracks, please!"

Sally took her turn. "I've topped up my RRSPs and named a beneficiary for my group policy at work, so the insurance proceeds won't have to go through probate if I die. And I'm still paying the full balance on my credit cards every month. No more interest payments for me."

We all listened to the crackling of the fire in silence for a few moments. I was looking at Dad's old navy bell from the ship he was captain of during WWII, thinking about how much I'd miss this place, when Sally asked if the family who'd been up to see it twice seemed anxious to buy.

"Not really," I answered. "It could be a year or two before we get a good offer, and until we do, I can't make a final distribution of Dad's estate."

"I think we could stand another summer like the one we just had," David remarked. "Alice and I have enjoyed spending time with all of you. Uncle Wayne was right, the real value of this cottage is wrapped up in the memories we all share. It's emotional, not financial."

"You're right," Sally said, adding that the memories will always belong to us, even if the cottage doesn't.

"Boy, I thought it was tough opening up this place without Dad last spring," I admitted, "but it's going to be even spookier closing it up for the winter."

"I know what you mean," agreed David. "By the way, what's on tap for tomorrow?"

"General cleanup," I answered. "And I believe it's your turn to straighten out the work shed."

"My turn? No way. Don't you remember last fall? Dad and I were clearing it out when we found that dead mouse. Remember how hard he was laughing when he chased Alice and Sandra around the deck with that thing!"

Appendix A

UNCLE WAYNE'S TOP ESTATE PLANNING TIPS

1. Have up-to-date wills.
2. Have up-to-date powers of attorney for both property and personal care.
3. Review your powers of attorney and will every few years.
4. Review your executor(s) every few years.
5. Determine if trusts may be of benefit to your family.
6. Consider a staged inheritance if you have young children.
7. Review your life insurance beneficiary designations on all your policies.
8. Review your beneficiary designations on all registered plans, such as group savings plans, RRSPs, TFSA and RRIFs, etc.
9. For RESPs, make them joint with your spouse, and name a successor subscriber in your will.
10. Consolidate your investments with one financial advisor.
11. Make sure you have enough life insurance to:

    • protect your family, and
    • if desired, create a family legacy, fund your favourite charity, and/or pay for estate costs.

12. Use term insurance for short-term needs, and permanent insurance for long-term or lifetime needs.
13. Consider permanent life insurance as a financial tool to reduce taxes and potentially create retirement income.
14. Create a digital estate plan.

15. Create a binder and/or use a secure cloud service for your essential estate documents, and make sure your executor knows how to access (see Appendix C).
16. Have the four essential family conversations (see Appendix B) with your children and/or parents:

    - the "estate documents" conversation with your executor, power of attorney, children and/or parents
    - the "eldercare" conversation with your children and/or parents
    - the "family legacy" conversation with your children and/or beneficiaries
    - the "next gen financial education" conversation with your children and/or beneficiaries.

17. Introduce your power of attorney and executor to your financial advisor, accountant, and lawyer.
18. Be wary of using joint ownership with anyone other than your spouse.
19. Consider "gifts" while alive for your family and/or donations to your favourite charity.
20. If you are a business owner, consider a secondary will for your business assets to avoid probate.
21. Prior to getting married or living common-law, consider a domestic contract (commonly referred to as a pre-nuptial or co-habitation agreement).
22. Pre-plan and perhaps pre-pay for your funeral.
23. Write down thoughts for your eulogy, which may include:

    - family tree
    - personal history
    - organized photos with names written on the back so the next gen will know who the people are!

24. Update and review your documents after a major life change or event such as marriage, birth, death, and divorce.

25. Some probate and estate tax minimizing strategies can have unintended consequences, so you will have to review all strategies with your insurance expert, accountant, lawyer, and financial advisor in conjunction with your entire estate plan.
26. Review and reflect on this checklist often.

Appendix B

THE FOUR ESSENTIAL FAMILY CONVERSATIONS

1. The Estate Documents Conversation

The estate documents conversation is a conversation you should have with your parents, children, executors, and powers of attorney to review and discuss the following key issues:

<u>With your parents:</u>

- Find out who their powers of attorney and executors are.
- Obtain copies of their wills and powers of attorney (or the location of the documents).
- Meet your parents' financial advisor(s).
- Obtain the listing of the location of their financial assets and the contacts for their bank, accountant, and lawyer (see Appendix C).
- Have a frank discussion on what they would want to happen if they were unable to make financial decisions for themselves.
- Have a frank discussion on what they would want to happen if they were unable to make health care decisions for themselves (also see Eldercare Conversation below).

<u>With your children:</u>

- Let them know who your executor and powers of attorney are.
- Provide copies of your wills and powers of attorney (or the location of the documents).

- Introduce your children to your financial advisor.
- Have a frank discussion on what you would want to happen if you are unable to make financial decisions for yourself.
- Have a frank discussion on what you would want to happen if you are unable to make health care decisions for yourself (also see Eldercare Conversation below).

With your executor and powers of attorney (if not your children):

- Let them know you have appointed them and provide them the documents.
- Confirm every few years that they are willing, able, and capable to act on your behalf.
- Provide to your executor/power of attorney the list of where your financial assets are and the contacts for your financial advisor, accountant, and lawyer (see Appendix C).
- Have a frank discussion on what you would want to happen if you are unable to make financial decisions for yourself.
- Have a frank discussion on what you would want to happen if you are unable to make health care decisions for yourself.
- Have the eldercare conversation with your power of attorney for personal care.

2. **The Eldercare Conversation**

With your parents and/or children, have a conversation about the potential strategies if a physical or medical setback were to occur. Issues you may want to discuss could include:

- What would the strategy be if they/you needed some extra help to continue to live at home?
  - o How is this to be financed? Is it in the financial plan?
- What is the strategy if they/you decided they needed to or simply wanted to move into a retirement home?
- Do they/you want or need to downsize their home?
- What is the strategy if only one spouse or parent needs care in a retirement home or long-term care facility?

- What would happen if both required care in a long-term care facility?
- What is the plan if dementia occurred for one or both spouses or parents?
- Have any funds or insurance been set aside to plan for extra care?
- Finally, create a list of all doctors and their contact information, and provide details of any health or insurance plans you may have in place.

3. The Legacy Conversation

The legacy conversation is a conversation you may want to have with your children and/or beneficiaries to discuss how your estate will be passed on. This will help you to:
- share your most important values with your children;
- let them know what you wish to happen as you age;
- potentially reduce confusion, discord, and family conflict;
- talk about any concerns you or they may have; and
- feel in control and let your children know that you have a plan.

Some of the potential topics to review could be:

- what's important to you in the legacy and wealth transfer process;
- the values you wish to pass on;
- the people who will have a leading role in your planning;
- health care issues, and the "eldercare" plan;
- why you may be using trusts versus an outright distribution;
- potential controversial issues, such as difference in amounts each child may be receiving;
- your charitable plan and strategy;
- your plans for your business.

Finally, let your children and beneficiaries know who all your advisors are.

4. The Next Gen Financial Education Conversation

This is a conversation you may want to have with the next generation to emphasize the importance of financial education and help them to be well equipped to handle their own financial affairs as they go through life's' transitions. Your financial advisor may be able to assist with this. Some key concepts and topics to review include:

- how to budget for post-secondary school;
- your first job and setting a lifestyle you can afford;
- simple budgeting and cash flow planning;
- understanding how taxes work;
- leasing versus buying a car;
- understanding your employer's benefit package;
- setting up a savings program;
- understanding the impact of interest charged on credit cards;
- the difference between good debt and bad debt;
- types of investments, such as high interest savings accounts, mutual funds, stocks, ETFs, etc.;
- types of savings vehicles, such as TFSAs and RRSPs;
- the financial impact of life's transitions, such as

  - getting married,
  - buying a home,
  - having children,
  - changing jobs or careers,
  - getting divorced,
  - caring for an elderly parent, and
  - safeguarding any inheritance they may receive.

Appendix C

PLANNING YOUR WILL AND POWERS OF ATTORNEY

Introduction

This document contains background information regarding the planning of your Will and Powers of Attorney.

Its purpose is to provide you with a further understanding of the subject matter and related issues, in order to assist you in making key decisions.

Your Will — an important part of your Estate Plan

We often talk about why you *need* a Will. Perhaps it would be more appropriate to talk about why you *want* a Will—an up-to-date Will that reflects your current circumstances and is properly planned and created.

Your Will is a key legal tool that is used to implement your estate plan should you die. It will govern how your assets are dealt with, to whom they are given and who has the responsibilities to look after these matters.

Should you die without a Will (or with a Will that does not distribute all of your assets), the "intestacy" laws would apply. These laws can produce arbitrary results that would likely not reflect your wishes. Without an appropriate Will, the administration of your estate would be more complex and costly. Moreover, by not having an up-to-date and carefully thought out Will, you can miss the opportunity to use strategies to minimize tax and avoid family disputes.

An out-of-date Will can be almost as bad as not having a Will. It may not reflect your current circumstances and it may not even deal with all of your assets.

Tax implications of dying

Planning to minimize taxes is an important objective in estate planning. This is because, in Canada, there are significant tax implications to dying.

When a person dies, he or she is deemed to sell all of his or her property for its value at that time. This fictional sale occurs immediately prior to death. Therefore, it is reported in the final tax return of the deceased person. This results in the following:

- The realization of any capital gains or capital losses (and the taxation of those gains)
- Registered plans, such as RRSPs and RRIFs, are taxed on their full value.

There are some exceptions, the most significant being where property is left to a surviving spouse (or partner) or to a qualifying spousal trust. In that case, the tax implications are deferred until the surviving spouse dies or until the property is sold. Another exception relates to the principal residence exemption that may be used to shelter the capital gain that is realized on a home or recreational property.

Probate fees or taxes are also a consideration. The amount of the fee or tax is calculated based on the size of the estate.

What will be in your Estate

One of the first steps in planning your Will is to determine which assets will form part of your estate and thus, be dealt with by your Will.

The determination of which assets will form part of your estate depends upon how you own your property and whether you have named beneficiaries in life insurance policies, registered plans and the like. Property that is jointly owned will not form part of your estate. Similarly, where a beneficiary has been named in a registered plan or in an insurance policy, the proceeds will go directly to that beneficiary and are not governed by your Will.

Thus, it is important to examine the relevant documents (e.g. title documents, account documents etc.) to confirm the owner and type of ownership and whether a beneficiary has been named.

Essential elements of a Will

A properly planned and drafted Will should take into account your current financial and personal circumstances and it should reflect your goals regarding the distribution and administration of your estate.

Here are the essential elements of your Will:

Naming Executors, Trustees and Guardians:

- Who would be best suited to handle your estate, and manage any trusts created in your estate? Your executors handle the administration of your estate and the trustees manage any ongoing trusts that may be created under your Will. They do not need to be the same people.
- If you appoint multiple individuals to act together, how should decisions be made?
- If there are minor children, who would you wish to name as guardians?

Distribution of your assets:

- Who should receive your assets? You should name primary beneficiaries and alternate beneficiaries in case the primary beneficiaries die before you.
- Are there certain of your assets that you should deal with specifically? For example, your business interests, home, family cottage, personal effects, etc.
- Should testamentary trusts be used—for children (and grandchildren) or to hold assets for a spouse (see the discussion below regarding testamentary trusts).

Using Testamentary Trusts in your Will

Testamentary trusts can be useful tools in estate planning. They can offer ways to save income tax and can also provide peace of mind by allowing assets to be managed by trustees on behalf of your beneficiaries.

A "testamentary trust" is a trust that arises on an individual's death, so it only becomes effective on the death of the person making the Will. The terms and conditions that apply to the trust are usually set out in the person's Will.

The most common forms of testamentary trusts are:

- **Spousal Trust**—which is for the benefit of the surviving spouse. Rather than assets being transferred directly to the surviving spouse, they are held in trust for the spouse. Such a trust requires that all income of the trust be paid to the surviving spouse, and no one other than the surviving spouse can have access to the capital of the trust while he or she is alive.
- **Trust for Child**—which is for the benefit of a surviving child (or grandchild). Assets are held in trust for the surviving child or grandchild instead of being transferred directly into the beneficiary's hands.
- The benefits of testamentary trusts include:
    - o **Reducing the total income tax payable** on the future income earned on the inheritance.
    - o **Helping to protect the beneficiaries' inheritance** from claims by creditors of the beneficiaries, family property claims and/or financial mismanagement by the beneficiary.
    - o **Ensuring that the testator's wishes and intentions will be respected** regarding the use of the inheritance.

Executors, Trustees and Guardians

Your executor is responsible for making funeral arrangements, safeguarding your assets and carrying out your wishes under the terms of your Will. Your trustee is responsible for administering any testamentary trusts which you set up under your Will. Often the executor and trustee are the same person, but you may appoint a different individual to perform each role.

You may appoint more than one executor, and more than one trustee. In that case, you should indicate how decisions are to be made.

Your choice of executor(s) and trustee(s) should be given careful consideration. They will make crucial decisions and it is important that they have good judgment and business sense as well as be able to relate well with the members of your family. You should also consider such factors as availability, willingness, age, health, residency, trustworthiness, impartiality and financial stability.

It may be appropriate to discuss the appointment with your executors and trustees and familiarize them with your affairs.

In your Will, you may appoint a guardian for any child who is under the age of 18. However, you should be aware, that the appointment of the guardians for your child must be approved by the courts whose primary concern is the best interests of the child. While this means that your wishes or preferences are not binding on the court, it is still valuable to include your preferred guardians in your Wills.

Your Powers of Attorney—key documents to manage your affairs

Your Powers of Attorney are the key legal tools used while you are still alive if you have become unable to look after your financial affairs or are unable to make decisions regarding your medical or personal care.

A Power of Attorney to manage property permits the appointed person(s) to deal with your assets. An "enduring" power of attorney is one that remains valid even after the individual granting the power becomes mentally incapable.

You may provide that the authority of the attorneys to act on your behalf only commences when you lose your mental capacity (sometimes referred to as a "springing" power of attorney), or alternatively that the attorneys may have authority with immediate effect.

A Power of Attorney to manage your health care authorizes the appointed person(s) to make personal or health care decisions on your behalf, should you become incapable of doing so.

You may revoke a Power of Attorney at any time while you are mentally capable.

Summary

There are a number of factors to consider as you plan your Will and Powers of Attorney. These include getting a clear picture of what is in your estate, identifying your beneficiaries, determining whether testamentary trusts will be used, and selecting your executors, trustees, guardians and attorneys.

Source: Assante Wealth Management

Appendix D

EXECUTOR CHECKLIST

The duties of Executor/Executrix/Liquidator in Quebec (referred to as the Executor throughout this document) require you to take on the responsibility of administering the estate and carrying out the last wishes of the deceased. The Last Will and Testament is the legally binding record of the wishes of the deceased regarding the distribution of his or her assets. If no Will exists, the deceased is considered to die intestate and your appointment by the Court as administrator of the estate will place the same responsibilities with you. In Quebec, the heirs of the estate will appoint a liquidator if there is no Will. This checklist lays out the main duties and responsibilities you will need to consider when handling an estate.

Step 1—Locate and review the Will

☐ Locate the Will and/or codicil and review to determine whether there are any special funeral directions.
☐ Talk to an estate lawyer (notary in Quebec) to obtain notarized copies of the Will.
☐ If the deceased died intestate, determine administrator and beneficiaries.
☐ Consider opening an estate bank account – this can help you keep track of money as it is received by the estate.

Step 2—Make Funeral Arrangements

☐ Assist in funeral arrangements if necessary.
☐ Obtain copies of the death certificate (you can get more than one) from the funeral director.

Step 3—Solicit Professional Counsel

☐ If it is referenced in the Will you can engage a lawyer, accountant or other professional to help you settle the estate. The cost of the professional is generally an expense of the estate.

☐ If it is not referenced in the Will, you may engage professional assistance, but beneficiary consent is advised.

Step 4—Notify Beneficiaries and Others

☐ Locate contact information for all beneficiaries.

☐ Notify beneficiaries of their inclusion in the Will.

Step 5—Identify and Secure Estate Assets

☐ Review immediate financial requirement of deceased's family. The following are potential sources of funds:

✓ Life insurance policies – only viable if the designated beneficiary(ies) are immediate family.

✓ Employment pay – if the deceased was an employee at the time of death, there may be some type of termination pay available (only viable if payable to a family member and not estate);

✓ Death benefit – there may be a death benefit through the employee's pension plan;

✓ Canada Pension Plan (Quebec Pension Plan) – if the deceased contributed to the CPP (QPP in Quebec), one can potentially obtain a lump-sum death benefit, while the survivor and children may be entitled to monthly payments.

☐ Arrange for safe custody of any valuables, such as cash, securities, jewellery etc.

☐ Stocks and bonds listing.

☐ Private company shares listing including share class ownership, tax returns, financial statements, articles.

- [ ] Real estate information.
- [ ] Location of any digital assets.
- [ ] If the deceased was a party to an agreement, such as a rental agreement, notify the landlord and arrange to terminate.
- [ ] Gather information regarding the deceased's RRSPs, RRIFs, annuities, pension and other type of retirement plan.
- [ ] Make a list of outstanding debts and liabilities.
- [ ] Notify CRA of the death.
- [ ] Notify Service Canada to arrange cancellation of Canada Pension Plan or Old Age Security payments.
- [ ] List and cancel driving license, magazine and newspaper subscriptions, cable, club memberships, telephone, internet, etc. and arrange for refunds as necessary.
- [ ] Cancel health insurance coverage.
- [ ] Notify life insurance companies of the death and include an original copy of the death certificate.
- [ ] Lock up the residence if the deceased lived alone and arrange for security and maintenance until arrangements are made according to the Will.
- [ ] If necessary, change the address with Canada Post to reroute any mail.
- [ ] Examine insurance coverage and insure estate assets (motor vehicle, house, furniture, jewellery, art, etc.) against perils and fire.
- [ ] Locate and obtain title documents for real estate, mortgages, share certificates, bonds, debentures, and guaranteed investment certificates.
- [ ] Arrange to review investment portfolio.
- [ ] Locate shareholder agreements, if any.
- [ ] Organize interim management for the business of the deceased, where applicable. If you, as the executor, decide to run the business, you must consider matters of personal liability.
- [ ] Arrange for listing of safety deposit box, if necessary.
- [ ] Contact credit card or loan companies to get the balance owing and arrange for payment and cancellation.

Note: Since renunciation is always a possibility, executors should be mindful of how involved they become in dealing with estate assets as they may be deemed to have accepted the responsibility of administering the estate.

Step 6—Submit Will for Probate

☐ Determine need for probate filing (this requirement varies by province so you should speak with the estate lawyer to determine the need for this tax filing). In Quebec, the holograph Will and the Will made in the presence of witnesses will need to be verified.

Step 7—Advertise for Creditors

☐ It is advised that executors advertise for creditors.

- The requirement to advertise for creditors varies from province to province so you should determine what the requirement is in your province.
- Some provinces may allow you to advertise online rather than in the local paper.

Step 8—Pay Debts and Complete Final Income Tax Returns

☐ Are the tax returns of the deceased up to date? Obtain prior year tax returns and notice of assessments/reassessments.

☐ If the taxpayer dies between January 1st and October 31st the T1 terminal return must be filed by April 30 of the following year.

☐ If the deceased passed away between November 1st and December 31st the T1 terminal return is due 6 months after the date of death.

☐ You may be required to file a return for rights or things – these are amounts that had not been paid to the deceased at the time of his/her death and that, had the person not died, would have been included in his/her income when received.

☐ The partnership or sole proprietorship stub period return.

- Return for income from a graduated rate estate – optional return for a deceased person who received income from a graduated rate estate (GRE). The GRE may have a fiscal period that does not start or end on the same dates as the calendar year. If the person died after the end of the fiscal period of the GRE, but before the end of the calendar year in which the fiscal period ended, an optional return can be filed for the deceased.
- Election to opt out of the regular spousal rollover under subsection 70(6.2) or the election regarding the spousal rollover of resource property.
- The election under subsection 164(6) to carry back a loss realized in the deceased's graduated rate estate's first taxation year to the terminal tax return to offset capital gains tax.
- The election to pay the deceased's tax in yearly installments under subsection 159(5).
- For estates with foreign assets, consider tax and disclosure reporting in foreign countries.

Step 9—Distribute Inheritances

- If a dependent relief claim is made against the estate the executor is not able to make distributions from the estate until the claim has been resolved. If the executor distributes the estate before the dependent relief claim has been resolved the executor could be held personally liable for the distributions, they made.
- If the executor is receiving compensation to settle the estate the executor compensation needs to be paid prior to distributing the proceeds of the estate. Executor compensation is taxable to the executor in the year it is received.
- If other professionals were engaged (i.e., lawyer, accountant etc.) they need to be paid prior to distributing the estate.
- The executor may want to consider obtaining a release from the beneficiary(ies) prior to distributing proceeds of the estate to the beneficiary(ies).
- Once all the tax returns have been filed it is necessary to obtain a clearance certificate from Canada Revenue Agency (CRA)

before the executor distributes any of the deceased's (estate's) property to the beneficiaries.

Step 10—Keep Accurate Records

- ☐ As an executor you are accountable to beneficiaries of the estate and should keep accurate records, complete accounting records,
- ☐ Invoices and receipts.
- ☐ In Ontario, you can also be audited for probate purposes for four years and by CRA for income tax purposes for three years, but the Income Tax Act requires that you retain records for six years after the return is filed.

Source Mackenzie Investments – Executor Checklist Published 11/18
Form 259457
www.mackenzieinvestments.com

Appendix E

INTESTACY THROUGHOUT CANADA

Published July 2017 – Source: CI Investments

Province	Spouse and one child	Spouse and children
Alberta	If all children are also children of surviving spouse, entire estate goes to spouse; if any of the children are not also children of the surviving spouse, the spouse gets the greater of $150,000 or 50% of the value of the estate, and the children receive the remainder of the estate.	
British Columbia	If all children are also children of the surviving spouse, first $300,000 + half of the remainder goes to the spouse; if any of the children are not also children of the surviving spouse, the first $150,000 goes to the spouse, 50% of the balance goes to the spouse, 50% of the balance to the children equally.	
Manitoba	If all children are also children of surviving spouse, entire estate goes to spouse; if any of the children are not also children of surviving spouse, greater of $50,000 or half of the estate goes to the spouse. Remainder of estate is split 50% between spouse and children.	
New Brunswick	Marital property to spouse; balance split equally.	Marital property to spouse; 1/3 balance to spouse; 2/3 of balance to children.
Newfoundland and Labrador	Split equally.	1/3 to spouse; 2/3 to children.
Northwest Territories and Nunavut	First $50,000 to spouse, balance split equally.	First $50,000 to spouse; 1/3 of balance to spouse; 2/3 of balance to children.

Nova Scotia	First $50,000 to spouse, balance split equally.	First $50,000 to spouse; 1/3 of balance to spouse; 2/3 of balance to children.
Ontario	First $200,000 to spouse, balance split equally.	First $200,000 to spouse; 1/3 of the balance to spouse; 2/3 of the balance to children.
Prince Edward Island	Split equally.	1/3 to spouse; 2/3 to children.
Quebec	1/3 to spouse; 2/3 to child.	1/3 to spouse; 2/3 to children.
Saskatchewan	First $100,000 to spouse; balance split equally.	First $100,000 to spouse; 1/3 balance to spouse, 2/3 balance to children.
Yukon	First $75,000 to spouse, balance split equally.	First $75,000 to spouse; 1/3 balance to spouse, 2/3 balance to children

Spouse in AB includes an "adult interdependent partner". In B.C. and SK this includes a common-law partner. In NS includes a domestic partner. In QC this includes a civil union couple. In NT/NU this includes a common-law couple but not a same-sex couple.

Specific rules regarding household furnishings and a spouse's ability to elect are unique in some provinces.

Division of property may be subject to matrimonial regime.

Appendix F

PROBATE FEES ACROSS CANADA

Probate Fees (For Estates Over $50,000)

Fee Schedule (Estates over $50,000) ★

Alberta	$275 to $525
British Columbia	$350 + 1.4% of portion >$50,000
Manitoba	$70 + 0.7% of portion >$10,000
New Brunswick	$100 + 0.5% of estates over $20,000
Newfoundland & Labrador	$60 + 0.6% of portion >$1,000
NWT	$215 to $435
Nova Scotia	$1,003 + 1.695% of portion >$100,000
Nunavut	$200 to $400
Ontario	1.5% of portion greater than $50,000
Prince Edward Island	$400 + 0.4% of portion >$100,000
Quebec	Nominal fee★★
Saskatchewan	0.7% of estate
Yukon	$140

★For some provinces and territories, different rates may apply to smaller estates (less than $50,000).

★★ Although Quebec does not levy probate fees, Wills (other than notarial Wills) must be authenticated by the Superior Court of Quebec. A nominal fee applies.

Source: BMO Wealth Management 2020

Appendix G

RISK MANAGEMENT PLANNING

To protect yourself, your family & your retirement due to unforeseen/unexpected events without damaging your lifestyle and savings.

Stage in Life	Wealth Management Concerns	Contingencies
Single—No kids	1. Protect yourself	Long Term Disability Insurance
	2. Protect your ability to earn an income	Critical Illness Insurance
	3. Protect your health	Health/Travel Insurance
	4. Protect your future	
Young Family	1. Protect ability to earn and income	Long Term Disability Insurance
	2. Protect your family	Life Insurance (income & debt)
	3. Cover off debt in an emergency	Critical Illness Insurance
	4. Protect family health	Health/Travel Insurance
	5. Tax efficient investing	Permanent Life Insurance
	6. Retirement planning	

Mature Family	1. Protect ability to earn and income	Long Term Disability Insurance
	2. Protect your family	Life Insurance (income & debt)
	3. Protect your retirement assets	Critical Illness Insurance
	4. Protect family health	Health/Travel Insurance
	5. Tax efficient investing	Permanent Life Insurance
	6. Efficient estate planning	Segregated Funds
Older Family	1. Protect your wealth	Critical Illness/Travel Insurance
	2. Efficient retirement income	Annuities
	3. Efficient estate planning	Segregated Funds/ Permanent Life Insurance
	4. Create a legacy	Permanent Life Insurance
	5. Care for yourself when you are unable to	Long Term Care Insurance

Source: Assante Estate and Insurance Services Inc.

Appendix H

INTERVIEW QUESTIONS FOR A FINANCIAL PLANNER

HOW TO INTERVIEW A FINANCIAL PLANNER

Financial planners can help you plan for retirement, find the best way to finance a new home, save for your child's education or simply help put your finances in order. Whatever your needs, working with a professional financial planner is a crucial step in helping you meet short-term and long- term goals that will help ensure your financial well-being.

Finding the right planner is extremely important because your choice will almost certainly affect the security of your financial future. The following questions will help you interview and evaluate financial planners to find a competent, qualified professional with whom you feel comfortable and whose business style suits your needs.

Don't be afraid to ask these and any other questions you feel need a full and open answer. Any professional will welcome them.

1. WHAT ARE YOUR QUALIFICATIONS?

Many people offering financial services call themselves financial planners. However, financial planning is a detailed, comprehensive process requiring hands-on experience and a strong technical understanding of topics such as personal tax planning, insurance, investments, retirement planning and estate planning – and how a recommendation in one area can affect the others.

In addition, in most provinces, there is no legislated standard in place for individuals who call themselves financial planners to obtain any credentials whatsoever. Some provinces have begun to introduce rules for those who use the title financial planner. However, it's important to make sure that your planner is appropriately trained, certified and held accountable to professional oversight – as Certified Financial Planner® professionals and Qualified Associate Financial Planner™ professionals are today.

- Ask the planner about his/her qualifications to offer financial advice and if, in fact, s/he is a qualified planner
- Ask what training s/he has successfully completed
- Ask what steps s/he takes to keep up with changes and developments in the financial planning field

- Ask whether s/he holds any professional credentials including CFP® certification or QAFP™ certification, which are recognized marks of competent, ethical and professional financial planners. You can verify a financial planner's certification status by searching for his/her name on the Find a Planner tool at findyourplanner.ca

2. WHAT EXPERIENCE DO YOU HAVE?

Experience is an important consideration in choosing any professional. Ask how long the planner has been in practice, the number and types of firms with which s/he has been associated, and how their work experience relates to their current practice. Inquire about what experience the planner has in dealing with people in similar situations to yours and whether s/he has any specialized training. Choose a financial planner who has at least one year of experience advising individuals on their financial needs.

3. WHAT SERVICES DO YOU OFFER?

The services a financial planner offers will vary and depend on their credentials, registration, areas of expertise and the organization for which s/he works. Some planners offer financial planning advice on a range of topics but do not sell financial products. Others may provide advice only in specific areas such as estate planning or taxation. Those who sell financial products such as insurance, stocks, bonds and mutual funds, or who give investment advice, must be registered with provincial regulatory authorities and may have specialized designations in these areas of expertise.

4. WHAT'S YOUR APPROACH TO FINANCIAL PLANNING?

The types of services a financial planner provides vary from organization to organization. Some planners prefer to develop financial plans encompassing all of a client's financial goals. Be sure to work with a planner who considers your overall financial goals, values and attitudes even if they specialize in a specific area such as taxation, estate planning, insurance or investments. As an example, an investment specialist's portfolio recommendations should consider your investment objectives and risk tolerance, but as well your cash flow needs, tax situation, risk management and estate goals. Ask whether the individual deals primarily with clients with specific net worth, levels of income or investable assets, and whether the planner will help you implement the plan s/he develops or refer you to others who will do so.

5. WILL YOU BE THE ONLY PERSON WORKING WITH ME?

It is quite common for a financial planner to work with others in their organization to develop and implement financial planning recommendations. You may want to meet everyone who will be working with you. Financial planners often work with other professionals, including the ones you already use, such as your lawyer and accountant.

6. HOW WILL I PAY FOR YOUR SERVICES?

Your planner should disclose in writing how s/he will be paid for the services they provide. Understand how your potential planner will be compensated and choose whatever model works best for you. Planners can be paid in several ways:

1. **From the cost of the product**: Some planners receive their compensation directly from the product manufacturer when you purchase a product through the planner. For example, their compensation is part of the management fee of the fund. In this case no money is exchanged between the client and the planner. Rather, the cost to the client is embedded in the cost of the mutual fund.
2. **Percentage of assets under management**: Some planners will charge a fee as a percentage of the assets they are managing or administering on your behalf.
3. **Fee-for-service**: Some planners charge an hourly or set fee for the service they provide.

7. HOW MUCH DO YOU TYPICALLY CHARGE?

While the amount you pay the planner will depend on your particular needs, the financial planner should be able to provide you with an estimate of possible costs based on the work to be performed. Such costs would include the planner's hourly rates or flat fees or the percentage s/he would receive as commission on products you may purchase as part of the financial planning recommendations.

8. WHO, BESIDES ME, BENEFITS FROM YOUR RECOMMENDATIONS?

Ask the planner – regardless of fee structure – if they have a written professional obligation to put your interests ahead of their own. For example, CFP professionals and QAFP professionals must annually attest to a code of ethics that clearly states your interests will always come first.

9. ARE YOU REGULATED BY ANY ORGANIZATION?

Financial planners who sell financial products such as securities and insurance or who provide investment advice must be regulated by provincial regulatory authorities. They may also subscribe to a code of ethics through a professional association. Others who are members of the accounting and legal professions are usually members of professional bodies that govern their fields. Planners who hold the CFP credential are subject to internationally recognized professional standards of competence, ethics and practice that are set and enforced in Canada by FP Canada™.

It is a fair question to ask if a prospective financial planner has ever been the subject of disciplinary action by any regulatory body or industry association. You can verify the answer by contacting the relevant organization. Ask the financial planner whether s/he subscribes to a professional code of ethics such as the FP Canada Code of Ethics for CFP professionals and QAFP professionals.

10. CAN I HAVE IT IN WRITING?

Ask the planner to provide you with a written agreement that details the services that will be provided. Keep this document in your files for future reference.

Source: FP Canada's website: Financial Planning for Canadians, June 2020: www.financialplanningforcanadians.ca/financial-planning/questions-to-ask-your-financial-planner

Acknowledgements

I'd like to thank the following people who made valuable contributions to the book:

For the original version:

Carl Frazer
Ron Rousseaux
Law Firm of Harris & Harris
Ruari Duffield – Interior Artwork

For this updated version:

Clark Craig
Derek Irwin-Lewis
Gillian Stovel-Rivers
Jackie Powers
Joan Cosby
Joe D'Aurizo
Lynda Tavares
Keith Masterman
Rachel Joudrie
Stuart Roberston
Tracy Irwin
Troy Rumpel

A special thanks to my sister, Sue Lumsden, for her valuable insight, editing, and guidance on both the original and updated version of this book.

A big thank you to Lynda Tavares who keeps me organized and on track each day!

"Do your job. Do your best. Never give up."
Roy Moore, A.H.S

About the Author

Jack Lumsden, MBA, CFP®, is a financial advisor with over twenty years of experience. He has enjoyed building a strong career and loyal client base. In addition to helping clients preserve and transfer their wealth, he focuses on those who are or will be making the transition from their working years to retirement with the need to develop a lifelong income and cash-flow strategy from the financial assets they have accumulated.

A lifelong resident of Burlington, Jack dedicates much of his spare time to staying active and coaching high school football. Spending time with family is another of his core values. He enjoys attending sports events with his son, Connor, and country music concerts with daughter, Paige, while he and his wife, Sandi, like to travel with friends and explore new destinations.

Jack's education includes a BBA from Wilfrid Laurier University (where he met Sandi), and an MBA from McMaster University. He is also a CERTIFIED FINANCIAL PLANNER® or CFP® professional.

How to Contact Jack Lumsden, MBA, CFP®

Jack Lumsden, MBA, CFP®
Senior Wealth Advisor
Assante Financial Management Ltd,

Phone: 905.332.5503
Email: jlumsden@assante.com
Web Site: www.jacklumsden.com

If after reading this book, you have any questions, or would like to arrange an appointment to review your current financial situation, please call or email us.

CPSIA information can be obtained
at www.ICGtesting.com
Printed in the USA
LVHW092318290921
699099LV00004B/117